Gratitude and Grit
The Life of Blessed Solanus Casey

Brother Leo Wollenweber, OFM Cap

franciscan
media®
Cincinnati, Ohio

This book was originally published by Servant Books
under the title *Meet Solanus Casey*.

Cover and book design by Mark Sullivan

LIBRARY OF CONGRESS CATALOGING-IN-PUBLICATION DATA
Wollenweber, Leo, 1917-2012
Meet Solanus Casey : spiritual counselor and wonder worker / Leo Wollenweber.
p. cm.
Includes bibliographical references. ISBN 1-56955-281-9 (alk. paper)
1. Casey, Solanus, 1870-1957. 2. Capuchins--United States--Biography. I. Title.
BX4705.C33573 W65 2002 271'.3602--dc21
2002009345

ISBN 978-1-63253-405-7

Published by Franciscan Media
28 W. Liberty St.
Cincinnati, OH 45202
www.FranciscanMedia.org

Contents

FOREWORD TO THE NEW EDITION ... *vii*

FOREWORD TO *Meet Solanus Casey* (2002) ... *xi*

ACKNOWLEDGMENTS ... *xiii*

PROLOGUE: *An Early Morning Caller* ... *xv*

ONE: *Family Roots and Formative Years* ... *1*

TWO: *A Boy Grows into Manhood* ... *9*

THREE: *The Capuchins Welcome a New Man* ... *17*

FOUR: *The Simplex Priest* ... *27*

FIVE: *The Seraphic Mass Association* ... *35*

SIX: *Ministry in Detroit* ... *43*

SEVEN: *"Deo Gratias"* ... *49*

EIGHT: *Witnesses to Holiness* ... *57*

NINE: *An Attempted Respite* ... *67*

TEN: *Secretaries and Other Colleagues* ... *75*

ELEVEN: *The Sacrifice of Self* ... *83*

EPILOGUE: *The Cause for Canonization* ... *93*

NOVENA PRAYER ... *101*

CANONIZATION PRAYER ... *103*

WISDOM FROM FR. SOLANUS ... *105*

NOTES ... *115*

A CHRONOLOGY OF THE LIFE OF
FR. SOLANUS CASEY, OFM CAP ... *119*

BIBLIOGRAPHY ... *125*

Foreword to the New Edition

There are many reasons why someone develops the need or desire to write about a saint and their life. Sometimes the holiness of an individual is so personally attractive and inviting that an author wishes to delve more deeply into their spirituality for their own growth in holiness. Other times the contribution or impact of a saint is so notable that a writer feels compelled to understand and explain why this singular life or ministry was so consequential. Then there are the disciples who might feel obliged to honor their mentors through such ventures. Sometimes the impetus comes from a whole community of devotees who believe that writing about their founder is essential for the survival and flourishing of whatever cause or community she or he inspired. While each of these motivations is laudable, sometimes even producing a spiritual classic, Br. Leo Wollenweber's impulse behind the creation of *Meet Solanus Casey* seems quite different.

While I never knew Blessed Solanus personally—he had died a decade before I entered the Capuchin community—I did know Br. Leo. We worked closely together on creating the Solanus Casey Center in Detroit in the late 1990s. In the process, Br. Leo's deep affection for Solanus and touching commitment to his charism became clear early on. His dedication to the man, and eventually to his cause for beatification, were born of a deep fraternal bond and an enduring friendship. It is difficult to explain the calculus that renders some folk friends and others not. It is equally difficult to explain why some members of a religious community like the Capuchins might develop a friendship beyond the fraternal bond expected by our profession. Several other friars besides Br. Leo offered their services as a secretary to Fr. Solanus, a position his superiors found necessary to establish given the legendary demands on his time through personal visits and the enormous volume of correspondence. There is little evidence, however, that any of the others who assisted him developed the bond with Fr. Solanus that Br. Leo did. One former secretary even admitted that he and Fr. Solanus had never even shared a heart-to-heart conversation.

There are some hints as to why this friendship developed. Like Fr. Solanus, Br. Leo had served as a "porter"—the traditional church name for someone who answers the door. Both men had also spent some time working in the world before religious life, and both were a little older when they entered the novitiate: Solanus twenty-six and Leo twenty-three. Even though Fr. Solanus had been ordained a priest and Br. Leo was a lay friar, both had acute experiences of minority in a community in which only those ordained priests who had been granted full faculties to preach and celebrate the sacraments were expected to rise to prominence. There was also resonance in their quite compatible personalities. Both of these Capuchin brothers were unpretentious and simple but with an unrelenting honesty about them. Another contributing factor had to be the context of their shared ministry at St. Bonaventure Monastery in Detroit in the early 1940s. It was an intense time for the aging and increasingly frail Solanus, eagerly assisted by the energetic and newly professed Leo, who was forty-two years his junior. Br. Leo was also Fr. Solanus's last assistant in Detroit. After twenty-one years at St. Bonaventure, Fr. Solanus was somewhat abruptly moved to New York in hopes of giving him a gentler life. Not surprisingly, the visitors and correspondence again piled up, prompting his transfer to the more rural Huntington, Indiana. Especially during the early years of these moves to supposed semi-retirement, Br. Leo became an important link to his beloved Detroit until Br. Leo himself was reassigned, only to move back to Detroit before Fr. Solanus's death in 1957.

It is true that Br. Leo was not Fr. Solanus's only friend in the community, or maybe even his best. Fr. Gerald Walker was the Capuchin provincial minister at the time of Solanus's death and offered the sermon at his funeral. Fr. Gerald's opening words of that sermon were: "Fr. Solanus was a man I loved dearly." It was reported that he often choked back his tears during this preaching. Fr. Solanus also had many dear friends outside the community. His deep friendship with his siblings was legendary. Beyond the immediate family his letters are filled with references to childhood friends, longtime acquaintances, and even "chums." On the other hand, none of his friends penned a biography of this beloved figure. That distinction belongs to Br. Leo.

The reason I dwell on this fraternal relationship in this new foreword is because rereading this gentle volume is like being introduced to a beloved friend. Over the decades since his death, multiple publications on the life of Blessed Solanus—some of them quite weighty and laden with scholarly footnotes—have appeared. These valuable contributions to the legacy of this celebrated door opener do not, however, diminish the value of this modest volume. To the contrary, given all the publications, DVDs, podcasts and broadcasts about Solanus that have and will appear, it seems all the more useful to have a thoughtful yet accessible guide to the breadth of his life and charism. This gentle volume, a modest reflection of both the author and the subject of the book, is an appropriate door opener for beginning the process of befriending the humble porter, Blessed Solanus. As I read it again, it reminded me of being introduced to one great friend by another.

When he died in 1957, Blessed Solanus was originally buried in the Capuchin cemetery behind St. Bonaventure Monastery. In 1987 his body was exhumed as part of the cause for his beatification and is now buried in the old north transept of the chapel of St. Bonaventure Monastery that currently extends into the spacious Solanus Casey Center. In the back-yard cemetery where Solanus Casey's earthly remains once rested there is a headstone marking this now-empty gravesite. Buried next to that spot is friend and advocate, fellow-porter, and brother Capuchin, Leo Wollenweber, who died in 2012. I imagine that Br. Leo's death kindled a celestial friendship of these two. This unassuming volume now opens a door for each reader, first to observe but then to enter into this ever-widening circle of friends and Blessed Solanus adherents. May our hearts only expand in devotion and generosity as we learn to echo the holy porter's constant refrain: "*Deo Gratias*! Thanks be to God!"

—EDWARD FOLEY, CAPUCHIN
vice-postulator for the cause of Blessed Solanus
Feast of Blessed Solanus, 2021

Sharing monastic or religious life is a good way to come to know people, to see them at their best and at their worst. Communal living reveals both one's strengths and virtues and one's faults and weaknesses. Br. Leo Wollenweber lived with Fr. Solanus Casey at St. Bonaventure Monastery in Detroit, Michigan, and grew to know him well. Whatever human failings he might have seen in this Servant of God, it was the good qualities he saw, the virtues, that impressed him.

It was, however, particularly in the close association with Fr. Solanus in his ministry with people outside the monastery that Br. Leo could observe the good and arrive at the conviction that here indeed was a truly holy man. For as Solanus's secretary, he had the added advantage of another perspective from which to take notice.

Meet Solanus Casey tells of the life of the Venerable Solanus Casey from an unobtrusively personal view. Going beyond the biographically factual, it includes firsthand stories and comments about Solanus the friar, the minister, the man.

Br. Leo has put this biography together well, writing with a simplicity and directness of style that makes it pleasant and easy to read. He has also provided an annotated list of other key works on Solanus and information about the process of canonization.

—Sister Bernadine Casey, SNJM

Acknowledgments

Although this short biography is based in part on personal recollections and on records available to me as vice-postulator for the cause of Fr. Solanus Casey's canonization, I am indebted to the inspiration of and research done by others who have written extensively about this holy Capuchin priest. Their works are listed in the bibliography at the end of this book.

I am grateful for the encouragement of all my Capuchin brothers, especially Fr. Daniel Fox, while Provincial Minister, and Br. Richard Merling, Director of the Father Solanus Guild. Their enthusiasm for the cause of Fr. Solanus has been my guide and support.

To Dean Campeau I give thanks for his computer expertise, which solved many difficulties. Finally, I give special thanks to Fr. Solanus's niece, Sr. Bernadine Casey, SNJM. Without her valuable editorial assistance this book would never have been written.

—Br. Leo Wollenweber, OFM Cap

Prologue

An Early Morning Caller

The monastery doorbell rang at two o'clock in the morning. Father Solanus ran down the steps to the door before anyone else was awakened. When he opened the door, a big, burly fellow blurted out, "Where's that Father Solanus? I want to kill him."

"Well, now," said Solanus, "we'll have to talk that over."

He ushered the man into the small office next to the door and sat down with him. The man said he was a communist and hated all priests. Solanus patiently listened to his angry tale of a dissolute life. Then Solanus gently spoke of God and God's love for all people, even sinners.

The man calmed down and gave up all thought of violence. Solanus told him to come back later in the day and make his confession. He returned, met another priest in the church who helped him to make a sincere confession, and after receiving absolution soon turned his life around.

Many people have said that after meeting Fr. Solanus and listening to him speak of God, they left with the feeling that a great weight had been lifted from their shoulders. I know that meeting Fr. Solanus had a profound effect on my life, and now I would like to share his life and goodness with people everywhere. This is the story of a man whom, once you have met him, you will never forget.

One

Family Roots and Formative Years

How merciful is the Good God in making us
dependent on one another.
—Fr. Solanus

Fr. Solanus Casey was just a simple man, a simple priest—not a man of letters, not a man of degrees—yet his thought reached to profound poetic and theological depths. Like a prophet, he was a man with a message for the future. That's what the bishop of Marquette, Michigan, the Most Reverend Thomas L. Noa, said when he learned of his death in 1957: "Father Solanus has a message for the people of God."

The message—always based in faith and trust in God, always consoling and encouraging, and bringing peace into troubled hearts—is embodied in the new and radical definition of religion Solanus devised: "Religion is the science of our happy relationship with, and dependence upon, God and our neighbor." He was profoundly aware of that relationship and dependence—that science—which continually unfolded in his own life. It began with a family that was steeped in Catholic spirituality and devotion.

STRONG CATHOLIC ROOTS

Bernard Francis Casey was born in a log cabin along the banks of the mighty Mississippi River, on the Wisconsin side. He was the sixth child in a family of ten boys and six girls born to Bernard James Casey and Ellen Elizabeth Murphy. Both Bernard and Ellen were born in Ireland in the 1840s and came to the United States after the dread famine years, the scourge of the Emerald Isle.

The elder Bernard Casey was born in 1840 at Castleblaney, County Monaghan. His parents were James Casey and Ellen McCaragher. James Casey was a stalwart and deeply religious man who, it is believed, died from wounds received while defending the Blessed Sacrament. A group of Orangemen attacked the church during parish devotions, and several Catholics were badly wounded in the fight.

After his father's untimely death, Bernard decided to try his fortune in America. He left home at the age of seventeen, together with a younger sister, to join relatives in Boston. His mother's parting words were, "Barney boy, keep the faith."

The two young people sailed from the port of Liverpool on the SS Curling and arrived in Boston on July 29, 1857, where they joined other family members. Bernard took up shoemaking in the Danvers, Massachusetts, area, which was the center of a flourishing shoe trade, and became quite skilled. His sister Ellen found work in the textile mills in the Portland, Maine, district. She quickly developed a friendship with a coworker, Ellen Murphy.

Ellen Murphy, the future mother of Solanus Casey, was the daughter of Michael T. Murphy from County Armagh. He had married Bridget Shields on September 20, 1827. Michael Murphy was among the early victims of the great famine, dying around 1847.

Left with her five children, Bridget Murphy returned to her home in Dungooley to be near her relatives. Eventually the family left Ireland to seek a better life in America. Ellen, who had been born on January 9, 1844, in Camlough, County Armagh, was eight years old at the time.

They sailed from Liverpool, England, on the Western Star and arrived in Boston June 20, 1852. They stayed with Shields relatives in Boston for a while, until Bridget, with her daughters Mary Ann and Ellen, found work in the textile mills near Portland, Maine. Her two older boys moved to Wisconsin to take up farming.

Love and Marriage

Bernard Casey had a significant visit with his sister Ellen in 1860. Together they went to a Fourth of July picnic at Biddeford, Maine. Also attending was Ellen Casey's good friend Ellen Murphy. It was love at first sight.

Bernard lost no time in proposing. But Ellen's mother thought she was too young, at sixteen, for the responsibilities of marriage and motherhood. Bernard would have to wait three years before he could claim his bride.

Bridget Murphy took Ellen with her to Hastings, Minnesota, to join her other daughter, Mary Ann, now married to James Moran. The Morans were expecting their first child, so Bridget and Ellen were needed there. After the baby arrived, Ellen began working in St. Paul for the wife of Ignatius Donnelly, the United States Senator from Minnesota.

Bernard tried to keep in touch with Ellen by mail but found their separation difficult. After three years he desperately asked his pastor to help him. The pastor in turn contacted Ellen's pastor. An opportunity arose when the Donnellys had to travel to Washington, DC. They arranged to take Ellen Murphy with them and to meet Bernard Casey there. Thus the two sweethearts were reunited.

Bernard and Ellen married on October 6, 1863, at St. James Church in Salem, Massachusetts. The Irish pastor of St. James, the well-loved Thomas Shahan, performed the ceremony, and the witnesses were William McChrystal and Jane O'Brien.

Bernard was now making shoes in Danvers for the Union Army. Before long he moved to Philadelphia with his bride and opened up his own shop. Their first child, Ellen, was born in Philadelphia on July 8, 1864.

Bernard contacted his brother Terrence, who had gone to Manchester, England, when Bernard came to America. He persuaded Terrence to join him in the shoemaking business. The two brothers opened a shop in New Castle, Pennsylvania, where many immigrants worked in the mines. A second child, James, was born to Bernard and Ellen in New Castle on August 14, 1865.

After the Civil War ended, Terrence and Bernard no longer had enough customers to keep their shoe business going. Terrence decided to go to Boston and study law. He completed his course and in time was admitted to the bar. Later he was appointed to the bench in Boston, where he served with honor as a respected judge.

Bernard, too, gave up the shoemaking business. He decided to find his future in farming.

LIFE IN THE COUNTRY

Ellen's brothers Owen and Patrick Murphy were already homesteading in Wisconsin, where good land was available. Their brother Maurice, the youngest in the family, was in Pennsylvania studying for the priesthood. On the Murphy brothers' advice, Bernard and Ellen bought eighty acres of good government land four miles south of Prescott, Wisconsin, in an area known as Oak Grove. Their property adjoined that of Owen and Pat Murphy.

It was here that five more children were born. One of them was Bernard Francis Casey, the future Fr. Solanus, born on November 25, 1870. He would be called Barney, like his father.

Three years later the Casey family moved to a larger farm at Big River in the Trimbelle area. There seven more children were born. Barney would spend ten of his formative years in this idyllic countryside.

In later years Fr. Solanus often reminisced in letters to the family about their happy days of childhood. He always gave thanks to God for their good parents and their dear family. In a letter to his brother Maurice in 1946, he paints a scene of those childhood days:

> When we think of the blessings of the past, since we went berry picking and picking hops and nuts and digging ginseng—when the "old field" was all we had open and the prairie chickens used to stage a picture like that of the first Paradise in the morning sun as they shook the dew from the great oaks...I have never seen a picture in Bible history or elsewhere so nearly like an earthly paradise as I remember that scenery to be—with deer in twos and threes and more stopping on the hillside or valleys to gaze at what we might be doing. No doubt what heightened the appreciation of those days was our innocence—and how the hawks were wont—as we would play on the grass stopping to watch them—to circle around and around in their upward flight. They seemed to me as they circled to the clouds to invite us to strive with them to get to heaven.[1]

The Idyllic Life

Barney Casey, Jr. grew up in a wholesome American family, rich in love and a solid Catholic faith. All the children had a love for sports and the outdoors. Hunting, fishing, swimming, and winter skiing and skating provided healthy exercise alongside their daily farm chores.

With ten boys in the family, they had their own baseball team, the "Casey Nine." Barney was the catcher and usually played without a glove. While the other boys also loved boxing, this was one sport that Barney would not join in because he couldn't bring himself to inflict pain on anyone.

Everyone did his or her part to keep the family united and happy. Helping their parents and each other came naturally to the children.

Bernard, Sr. had a job for each of the boys, keeping the farm in good order and the animals healthy.

Their mother had the help of the girls around the house. But even the boys took turns babysitting the infants. Barney was glad to watch over the little ones. He would keep the babies occupied and content by playing his harmonica.

In later years Solanus would fondly recall those happy days when counseling people who were experiencing family trials. To parents he would always emphasize the value of faith and family prayer as the real source of happiness in this "valley of tears."

Daily life on the farm was full of surprises and much excitement for young Barney. One day, coming home from the pasture, their dog Rover wandered off to the woods and was attacked by a vicious wildcat. The boys tried to rescue Rover, but the cat kept them at bay and hung on to Rover.

Barney saw his chance. He picked up a large stone and circled around until he was behind the struggling animals. He was able to get close enough to fling the rock at the cat's head, and the blow killed it. In triumph the boys brought back the carcass—good for a ten-dollar bounty.

Meeting Trials

Of course, life on the farm was not always easy. The demands of farm work often interfered with schooling, and these interruptions hindered Barney's elementary education. Sometimes the boys had to practice their lessons or catechism while tending the cows in the pasture. The brothers might get into some mischief and then have to chase after wandering cows, to the neglect of their books.

The Caseys, like their neighbors, experienced lean years when crops were not so good or when bad weather delayed planting and harvesting. There were other natural disasters that could strike fear into their hearts. In a letter to his sister Margaret many years later, Solanus vividly described a prairie fire that had threatened their home:

It was on a Sunday, when Papa and Jim had gone to church, when we saw the black clouds of smoke rising from the far side. The wind was pretty strong too, and poor dear Mother seemed quite anxious—giving instructions what to do and getting ready for what must have looked probable, a burn-out.

Ellie scratched a little "hoe-mark" out in front of the house and sprinkled holy water in it about halfway down to the barn. By this time the fire was crackling through the grass and brush...and the smoke rolled over our heads in thick dark clouds. Then the barn took fire, some ten rods east of the house, and we all went down, carrying some bedclothes, to the lone tree that stood in the middle of the four-acre field....As we stood huddled together under said lone tree...I heard Mother saying in accents of relief, "Thanks be to God! Some of the neighbors have come and let the pig out." We saw it running for safety. Papa and James got home shortly after, and some of the neighbors came to sympathize with us.2

Another letter speaks of the tragedy that struck this happy home in November 1878, when two of the girls, Mary Ann, aged twelve, and three-year-old Martha, died during the diphtheria epidemic. Young Bernard also contracted the disease, which left him with a weak, wispy voice for the rest of his life.

A LIFE OF PRAYER

The Irish Catholic faith was nourished above all else in the Casey home. This was something that Barney Casey never forgot, and something for which he ever gave thanks to God.

Family prayer was a daily custom brought over from Ireland by Bernard and Ellen Casey and faithfully taught to their children. Solanus often described the way their father would get them together in the evening by calling out, "Prayer, boys, prayer!"

Then their mother would begin the rosary, and all took turns leading the decades. From his youth, Barney Casey developed a love for the rosary and resolved to say it every day. He remained faithful to this practice throughout his life and recommended it to others.

For Sunday Mass the family had to alternate going to church because they were too many for their small wagon to carry. Half would go on one Sunday and the other half the next week. But those who stayed home would have their own devotions. They read the Sunday Gospel, and their father or mother would lead them in prayers from the Mass.

In 1883, before his thirteenth birthday, Barney spent a few weeks in Hudson, Wisconsin, at St. Patrick's Church. There the pastor, Fr. Thomas A. Kelly, gave him instructions for his First Holy Communion. Barney eagerly took to heart the simple catechism lessons and Bible history.

God found fertile ground in the Casey family in which to plant the seed of vocation. Attending midnight Mass one Christmas Eve, even before his First Communion, little Barney wondered in his heart if he could ever be a priest. This desire grew little by little.

Eventually his older brother Maurice went off to the seminary because he seemed the one chosen for the priesthood. Yet Barney secretly wondered if there could be two priests in the family. His hopes were dashed when, after a year or two, poor Maurice had to return home because of a nervous condition that made study too difficult. Barney had always looked up to Maurice, and now he felt that if Maurice couldn't make the studies, how could he?

However, the little seed planted by God in young Barney's heart would continue to mature. Near the end of his life he wrote to a friend who was struggling against all odds to open a cancer hospital: "God, who loves tiny beginnings, will know as He always does know, how and when to provide developments."

Two

A Boy Grows into Manhood

*Oh, what God must have ahead of us if we
only leave all to His planning!*
—Fr. Solanus

As he grew into his teens Barney eagerly participated in school and
the country life of his time. The family moved to a 345-acre farm in St.
Croix County, Wisconsin, bordering on the Willow River, about eight
miles from Hudson. They were halfway between two small mill towns,
Burkhardt and Boardman, and the Chicago and Northwestern Railway
tracks went along the edge of their property. Here they had a large house
with three bedrooms upstairs and one downstairs, besides a large living
room and a newly built kitchen. This was home for the Caseys from 1882
to 1891 and the birthplace of their last two children, Grace and Mary
Genevieve.

This property had many advantages. Dry Dam Lake was within its
boundaries, so with the lake and the river the Caseys had good swimming and fishing. In the winter the frozen lake and stream were ideal for
skating, another healthy pastime. Of course, more acreage meant more
crops and more work for ten growing boys and their father.

Bernard Casey, Sr. was a good farmer but not a taskmaster. He knew how to balance work and recreation. The Casey home was a lively place, and evenings were happy with spirited discussions and song.

Amid the Irish humor and banter, tempers sometime flared up, too. Young Barney was no exception. Once when exasperated he threw a fork at one of the girls. His father sternly corrected him with the promise of a few lashes if he ever did that again, something that he never forgot. In later years as a Capuchin novice, he wrote in his notebook that he had to learn self-control.

First Jobs

These were years when young Barney Casey made good progress at the Burkhardt elementary school in spite of the interruptions for farm work. He took a special interest in the school debates and led a winning team a few times. He seemed to lean toward literature and poetry and showed promise in these studies.

But these also were years when the crops sometimes failed and hard times threatened, so Barney, Jr. considered how to help his parents through the crisis. He decided to look for work in nearby Stillwater, Minnesota, even though it meant he would have to interrupt his schooling.

Stillwater, across the St. Croix River, was a center for logging operations. Barney first found work sorting the logs on the river with other men. It was dangerous work for a skinny youth, but Barney was determined and courageous.

Fortunately he had two uncles in the city, and he could count on their help. Fr. Maurice Murphy was the pastor of St. Michael's Catholic Church, where Barney had received the sacrament of confirmation in 1883 along with his brother John. His uncle Pat Murphy was a guard at the Stillwater State Prison. While in Stillwater Barney lived with his Uncle Pat and Aunt Mary Murphy.

Uncle Pat eventually got him a job as a part-time guard at the prison. There Barney made friends with some of the prisoners, among whom were Jim and Cole Younger, members of the notorious Jesse James Gang. When Barney left to seek other work, Cole gave Barney a little wooden chest that he had made.

By means of these jobs Barney was able to help the family with needed cash. At the same time he kept close to the family, going home whenever he could.

There was much to draw the young man back home. The teenaged Caseys and their friends were a lively group who loved music. They had their local entertainments, and barn dances were a favorite.

On one occasion a family visitor left a violin with the Caseys, and Barney picked up a little fiddling on his own. He was good enough to come into demand for the local dances. Later on as a Capuchin he would sometimes play his favorite hymns for the community. However, as he had never studied music, his confreres did not appreciate his fiddling.

About this time it seems that Barney became very friendly with a girl his age who lived on the farm next to the Caseys. Rebecca Tobin and Barney soon were seeing a lot of each other, and Barney finally proposed. But Rebecca's mother thought she was too young to be thinking of marriage. She immediately packed her daughter off to a girls' school in St. Paul.

It was the end of Barney's romance, and now his life took a new turn. Stillwater was just installing electric streetcars, so Barney, who was quite enterprising, applied for a job and became one of the first streetcar conductors in the Midwest. He would follow this novel occupation into Appleton, Wisconsin, and then finally to Superior, Wisconsin, when the "newfangled" streetcars were introduced there.

DIVINE APPOINTMENT

Superior had a promising future as a boomtown at that time, said to rival Milwaukee. Barney saw good prospects for his brothers and sisters, so he persuaded the whole family to give up the farm and relocate in Superior. The move proved beneficial to the Caseys, because good jobs were available and the opportunities for higher education came within reach for all.

By this time Barney was training other men for streetcar jobs, and he had become a motorman. One day as he was driving through a rough section of town, destiny rode with him. A commotion on the track ahead forced the car to a sudden stop. A crowd had gathered around a young woman lying on the tracks. Barney jumped off to see a sailor brandishing a knife over the girl's bleeding body. Police overpowered the man, and help arrived for the girl.

The awful scene made a profound impression on Barney Casey. He spent the evening praying for the poor woman and her assailant. The thought of such violence in society made him think again of offering himself for the service of God in the Church in order to help counteract the evil. He felt that he must do something more with his life.

At this time Barney came under the influence of a saintly Franciscan priest in Superior, Fr. Eustace Vollmer, spiritual director for the Third Order or Secular Franciscans. Both Casey parents belonged to the Secular Franciscans, so young Barney also may have joined the order. He told Fr. Eustace of his desire to serve God as a priest. Fr. Eustace advised him to see his pastor, Fr. Edmund Sturm, at Sacred Heart Parish.

Barney would be entering the seminary at the high school level. The seminary recommended by his pastor was the Diocesan Seminary of St. Francis de Sales in Milwaukee, also known as the "German Seminary," where most of the classes were taught in German. That this was the same seminary where his brother Maurice had failed to make the grade some years before did not seem to discourage Barney in his decision.

Adjusting to Seminary

Young Bernard Casey now faced new challenges, which he met with his customary single-mindedness. Seminary life was a totally new experience of order and discipline, strictly enforced by the sound of bells. Bernard quickly adapted to it. Little did he foresee that in time, his life would be regulated in the same way by bells at a monastery office.

He had to adjust to work and study among youths much younger than himself. His experience with younger siblings somewhat prepared him for this. Among the students he was well liked, looked upon as an older brother who could bring calm into sudden quarrels with a few gentle words and restore friendships that had become strained

There were bouts of sickness and recurring spells of quinsy sore throat that would plague him many times during the next four years, and these certainly must have interfered with his studies. He also took on some extracurricular activity, becoming the seminary barber in order to earn something toward his tuition. This would limit his study time, which also would tell on his marks. During the first couple of semesters his grades were good. He was an earnest student and tried his best. His marks for conduct and application were always "1," and he passed all tests with good marks. During his second year a slight falling-off began to show in his grades, which was attributed to his problems comprehending the German language. This language problem did not yet signal failure.

In his twenty-fourth year Barney went home to Superior for vacation. His brothers now had a dairy farm, and he joyfully pitched in to help with chores. He never seemed to lose his love for the farm and country. Although his later life as a Capuchin was spent in bustling cities, he would find joy in a little work in the monastery gardens whenever he had leisure time.

Some of his letters reveal the sense of God's presence that he found in nature. In a letter to his sister Margaret from Yonkers in 1916, he wrote of the beautiful Hudson Valley:

> Surely the natural scene now before me when I turn my head to look
> at it is as picturesque as any scene of long ago. But what is nature in

the light of the supernatural, and what are natural blessings in the
light of immortality?

When he returned to school after the pleasant visit home, his marks came
up again. During the fall of 1895 he entered Class Five, equivalent to the
first year of college. The second semester saw his grades go down once
more, and in some classes he barely made passing marks.

Finally his seminary superiors had to advise him that he likely would
not succeed in the diocesan seminary. The authorities did not entirely
discourage him, but they suggested that he might have a vocation to a
religious order.

Perhaps his intense spirituality was a sign of a more contemplative religious calling.

Bernard was conscientiously concerned with serving God in any way
God might call him, but this time he returned home discouraged and
unsure of God's plan for him. He prayed for God's grace and guidance,
but the future seemed dark and uncertain.

Our Lady Shows the Way

Throughout the summer and fall of 1896, Bernard prayed often that he
might discover God's will for his life. He asked himself, "Does God want
me to become a priest?"

He sought out Fr. Eustace Vollmer, whose spiritual advice had guided
him before. The kindly Franciscan reminded Bernard of the suggestion
the seminary superiors had made: Try some religious order. Fr. Eustace
advised him to write to the provincial superiors of the Franciscans, the
Jesuits, and the Capuchins, all well-known throughout Wisconsin.

When Bernard received favorable replies from all three orders, he was
in a quandary. While at the seminary in Milwaukee he had visited the
Capuchins, who led St. Francis Parish and Monastery in the city. Their

austere appearance, with their long beards and sandaled feet, did not appeal to him. What little he knew of the Franciscans and Jesuits did not seem to attract him to their way of life either.

The approaching Feast of the Immaculate Conception seemed to be an opportune occasion to seek Our Lady's help. He asked both his mother and his sister Ellen to join him in a novena of prayer for God's grace and guidance.

On the day of the feast, December 8, after receiving Holy Communion, he distinctly heard Our Lady tell him, "Go to Detroit." The nature of the vision or mystical experience he never revealed, but it did give him the answer he was seeking. "Go to Detroit" meant the Capuchins, because they had their headquarters and novitiate there.

He never for an instant questioned Our Lady's directive. He immediately began to make arrangements to follow her inspiration. The time was just before the Christmas holidays, and the family urged him to wait and celebrate the great feast with them at home. But by December 21 he was ready to embark on the new venture.

Three

The Capuchins Welcome a New Man

There is no peace for the rational creature except in the
willing service of its Creator.
—Fr. Solanus

After a three-day journey by train through a steady snowstorm, Bernard Casey finally arrived at St. Bonaventure Monastery in Detroit on December 24, 1896, Christmas Eve. It was an exhausted young man the friars welcomed to the monastery. Shown to a small room containing a bed, a desk, and a chair, Bernard sat down and wondered what Our Lady had brought him to. He stretched himself out on the bed and fell fast asleep.

At midnight he was suddenly awakened to the sound of bells and singing and the pungent smell of incense. The friars were being awakened for the midnight Mass of Christmas. Jumping up refreshed and wide-awake, Bernard joyfully joined the singing procession to the chapel. In years afterward he often told of the serene happiness he felt that holy night.

The Novice

Barney quickly adjusted to the monastery routine. As the new year dawned, the novice master seemed satisfied with the new candidate. He decided to invest him with the holy habit of St. Francis on January 14. But now Bernard felt some misgivings. Darkness troubled his soul, and he must have experienced a temptation to leave. Among some memorable notes he wrote on the flyleaf of his little copy of the Franciscan Rule is, "January 13, 1897. Dark indeed."

Years later he mentioned this spiritual struggle, and the peace that followed it, in a letter to one of his brothers: "The moment I entered the Friars' Chapel to receive the habit, the struggle ceased and never troubled me again."

On January 14, 1897, he was clothed in the brown habit and white cord of a Capuchin and given a new name, Friar Francis Solanus. His patron was the great Spanish missionary to Peru St. Francis Solano, a Franciscan priest who loved the poor native children and called them to catechism with his violin. As the Capuchins in Detroit had another friar called Francis, this new friar became known simply as Solanus. He would have his patron's missionary heart and zeal, but his mission would be in his own land.

In religious life, the novitiate is a serious time of testing and trial. The novice must get accustomed to new demands on his generosity and self-discipline and come to know himself in the light of those demands. The order takes time to study the novice to see if he has the necessary qualities to persevere in observance of the vows of poverty, chastity, and obedience.

While Bernard's mature age might have made him more certain of this calling, nevertheless he had to pass the Capuchin novitiate test and be carefully scrutinized by his superiors. Fortunately, Frater Solanus came under the direction of Fr. Gabriel Messmer, a novice master of exceptional spirituality and fatherly kindness, with great insight and interest in the welfare of the novices.

This was a time when Solanus would get a thorough grounding in the Franciscan Rule and Capuchin spirit, as found in the order's Constitutions. Years later he could write, "How can we ever be [as] grateful as we ought to be for such a vocation to the Seraphic Order of the Poverello of Assisi?"

One of the most significant lessons of the novitiate was to learn the real meaning of the term "Friars Minor," which St. Francis gave to his followers. It means that Franciscans must consider themselves the least, not only of religious but also of all people. At the same time it means that they must be brothers to one another and to all creation. Solanus would grow in this spirit more and more throughout his life.

FIRST WRITINGS

In the novitiate Solanus began writing spiritual notes for himself in a little notebook. Sometimes he copied quotations from various spiritual authors, and other times he noted his own spiritual reflections. Meditating on St. Bonaventure's steps to perfection he jotted down the following:

MEANS FOR ACQUIRING THE LOVE OF GOD

I.   Detachment of oneself from earthly affections. Singleness of purpose!

II. Meditation on the Passion of Jesus Christ.

III. Uniformity of will with the Divine Will.

IV. Mental Prayer—meditation and contemplation.

V.   Prayer—ask and it shall be given to you (Matt. VII-7).

Then he noted:

TO PRESERVE GOD'S PRESENCE

I.   Raise your heart to Him by frequent aspirations.

II. Make a good intention at the beginning of each work and frequently during its execution.[1]

Gradually Solanus became more centered and abandoned to God. He learned to avoid excessive rigidity and a certain scrupulosity that he had suffered for a time. His spirituality was not only interior; it also became directed in charity to his fellow novices. This trait of fraternal charity to all his confreres distinguished him also in future years.

On July 14, 1897, Solanus's novitiate test was over, and he was admitted to temporary profession of the three vows of poverty, chastity, and obedience. Nevertheless, his superiors seemed to have some concern about Solanus's future studies. At this point he was asked to sign a statement about his intentions. The following "Attestation" was found in his provincial file after his death:

> I, Frater Solanus Casey, declare that I joined the Order of the Capuchins in the Province of St. Joseph with the sure intention to follow thus my religious vocation. Although I would wish and should be thankful [to] be ... admitted to the ordination of a priest, considering the lack of my talents, I leave it to my superiors to judge on my faculties and to dispose of me as they think best. I therefore will lay no claim whatsoever if they should think me not worthy or not able for the priesthood, and I always will humbly submit to their appointments.[2]

Already he was coming to learn the degree of humility that God would ask of him.

CAPUCHIN STUDENT

Now he and his four classmates were Capuchins, but years of hard study awaited them before they would reach the priesthood. From Detroit they journeyed to St. Francis Monastery in Milwaukee, Wisconsin, site of the Capuchins' major seminary.

Fr. Anthony Rottensteiner was the director of students. He had been ordained for the diocesan clergy in Germany before joining the American

Capuchins. His brilliant record as a student in Germany gave promise of a great career, but he felt a strong desire to dedicate himself to mission work. His particular concern was the German-speaking immigrants in America.

In 1867, Anthony applied to the young Capuchin foundation in the United States. The American Capuchins were in great need of a true scholar to direct their seminary. Fr. Francis Haas and Fr. Bonaventure Frey, the two founders of the Capuchin Province of St. Joseph, soon noticed Anthony's impressive talents for teaching. Thus Anthony began a long career of teaching while still a novice. His valuable gift for judging the fitness of candidates for the priesthood would prove providential for Solanus Casey.

When Frater Solanus came to St. Francis Monastery to begin his studies anew in Milwaukee, he discovered that his classes would again be taught mainly in German and Latin. He had had a problem with these languages while at the diocesan seminary. Solanus struggled doggedly with the language handicap, as did another student classmate of Irish parentage, John O'Donovan.

At first his scholastic rating was passing or a little below average. Solanus's steadfast determination may account for the extra consideration that Fr. Anthony showed toward him in class. The teacher would phrase his questions in such a way that Solanus could readily grasp them and be able to formulate the answers. No one criticized the director; the students and faculty all loved Solanus for his genuine spirituality, humility, and very evident love of God. His fidelity to the Franciscan rule and every duty made a deep impression on his confreres and earned their esteem.

Fr. Boniface Goldhausen, once a younger classmate of Solanus, characterized him as a "quiet, recollected, and very observant cleric." In 1970 he wrote these impressions of Solanus the student:

> If playing a game like checkers, he always preferred that his oppo-
> nent would win. At his work he was very exact and painstaking. On
> feast days, to decorate the altar he would put out extra candles and
> bouquets of flowers. He would then step back and look at it. If they
> were not exactly perfect, he would move a candle or bouquet until
> they were right where he wanted them. They had to be symmetrical.[3]

While his classmates might have considered him quite exacting in his
work and spiritual exercises, Solanus himself was aware of many deficien-
cies. He wrote in his notebook, "Patience, therefore, with your faults.
Beware of silent criticism."

Another note gives evidence of Solanus's concern about his spiritual
advancement:

> Traits of Saintly Characters consist of three things:
> 1. Eagerness for the Glory of God;
> 2. Touchiness about the interests of Jesus;
> 3. Anxiety for the salvation of souls.

Solanus was also beginning to manifest the overriding sense of concern
for others that would distinguish his later years of service to the poor and
suffering. An entry in his notebook is a quotation from Pope Clement
XIV addressing the need to be concerned about the poor and one's
neighbor. He later wrote to his sister Ellen urging her to "admonish little
Owney [their brother] not to neglect the most salutary [deed]—alms-
giving for the poor and orphans."

Preparing for Ordination

Solanus's progress in theology, however, continued to concern his superiors. While a student's fitness for the priesthood was not based only on
his scholastic record, this certainly was an important factor.

As the faculty began to question this, the wise Fr. Anthony made an
extraordinary prediction: "We shall ordain Frater Solanus, and as a priest,

he will be to the people something like the Curé of Ars." This was a reference to St. John Vianney, who also failed in his studies but became a holy director of souls.

Yet the superiors still had their concerns. Again Solanus was asked to make a declaration of intent before making his final profession of vows in July 1901. His statement, this time written in German, was as follows:

> I, Frater Solanus Casey, having entered the order with a pure intention and of my own free choice, wish to remain in the Order, and I therefore humbly ask for admission to solemn profession. However, since I do not know whether, as a result of my meager talents and defective studies, I am fit to assume the many-sided duties and serious responsibilities of the priesthood, I hereby declare (1) that I do not want to become a priest if my legitimate superiors consider me unqualified; (2) that I still wish to be able to receive one or other of the orders, but will be satisfied if they exclude me entirely from the higher orders. I have offered myself to God without reservation; for that reason I leave it without anxiety to the superiors to decide about me as they may judge best before God.[4]

Solanus was permitted to take final vows with his classmates on July 21, 1901. Although the following school year saw his grades slipping a little, the superiors also allowed him to receive the minor order of tonsure, which at that time was a mark of the clerical state.

When his class was ready for ordination to the subdiaconate, Solanus was among them. On December 8, 1903, he was ordained a subdeacon at St. Francis de Sales Seminary Chapel in Milwaukee.

In a letter to his sister Ellen in February 1904, Solanus indicated that there might be some questions regarding his reception of the other orders, but he remained open to whatever decision the superiors would make: "I will probably be ordained deacon and priest before August. May the Holy

Ghost direct my superiors in their decision in this regard, and may His Holy Will in all things be done." Under his signature he added the word, "Resignation."

Joy in Submission

In spite of his efforts during the following months, Solanus's marks did not improve significantly. Of the six men in his class, three students showed "very good" or "good and average" marks. The other three—Solanus Casey, John O'Donovan, and Damasus Wickland—had mostly "average and passing" marks. It was decided that the latter three would be ordained as "simplex priests," that is, without faculties to hear confessions or preach doctrinal sermons.

Perhaps Solanus could have received full faculties had he pushed for it, as did Fr. John later on. Instead he joyfully accepted the limitation as God's will. He never received permission to give absolution in the sacrament of reconciliation nor did he ever give evidence of disappointment or resentment. This complete acceptance of his superiors' disposition in his regard was yet another indication of his growth in the virtue of humility.

All six classmates were ordained to the holy priesthood on Sunday, July 24, 1904, in St. Francis Parish Church. The new archbishop of Milwaukee, Sebastian Messmer, presided. He was the brother of Solanus's former novice master, Fr. Gabriel Messmer. It was indeed one of the happiest days of Solanus's life.

One week later, on July 31, 1904, to the great joy of his parents and brothers and sisters, Solanus celebrated his first Solemn Mass at St. Joseph's Parish in Appleton, Wisconsin. This was the closest Capuchin church for the Caseys, though they still had to travel two hundred miles. As Solanus wrote years later, it was a memorable day for all the family. It was the first time he had seen his mother in eight years, and his father wept for joy that God had blessed his family with a priest.

His brother Maurice, now working for the railroad, spoke with Solanus as they walked in the monastery garden. Recalling his early seminary days, Maurice exclaimed, "By George, I think I'll try it again." Maurice did return to studies in 1905 at St. Jerome College in Berlin, Ontario. In 1907 he entered St. Paul Seminary in St. Paul, Minnesota, and he was ordained for the diocese of Helena, Montana, on June 9, 1911.

Their younger brother Edward had entered the seminary at St. Paul in 1903. Maurice had offered to pay his brother's tuition with the hope that Edward might succeed where Maurice had failed years earlier. Edward was ordained in 1912 and had a long career as an educator and pastor in St. Paul and as a missionary in the Philippines. Thus three Casey brothers came to hear God's call to serve his Church as priests. The firm Catholic roots of this family were to bear abundant fruit.

Four

The Simplex Priest

If you can honestly humble yourself,
your victory will be certain.
—Fr. Solanus

Fr. Solanus's first assignment was to the Capuchin Parish of the Sacred Heart in Yonkers, New York. This once-German parish now had an influx of Irish families. These welcomed the new priest named Casey.

The superior at Sacred Heart was Fr. Bonaventure Frey, the former provincial superior who had accepted Bernard Casey into the Capuchin novitiate in Detroit seven years earlier. Now, as his pastor, he wondered what to do with this new "simplex priest." He assigned him first as sacristan and director of the altar boys and then as porter or doorkeeper.

Usually these were jobs for brothers, the unordained friars. But Solanus did not find the work demeaning. To him it was a privilege to have the care of the church and the altar. Working so close to the Blessed Sacrament enabled him to foster an intense devotion to the Eucharist. There before the "Eucharistic King" he would remember the needs of all his friends and family, and especially the needs of the sick and the poor.

The 'Holy Father' at Work

At the monastery door and in the office, Solanus came into contact with a great many people and their humble concerns. His heart went out to all. He had such empathy, together with a spirit of devotion to and confidence in God, that soon, when people were sick, they would come to the monastery and ask for Fr. Solanus.

Some Italian immigrants had moved into the parish, and they heard of Fr. Solanus. When they had sickness in their families, they would go to the Petrosino home and ask little Carmella Petrosino to go ask the "Holy Father" to come and bless the sick. Carmella was the interpreter because Solanus could not converse in Italian.

Walking along with Solanus one day, Carmella told him of her desire to be a sister. She did not think it possible because her family was very poor, but he assured her that she would become a Sister of St. Agnes, the order that taught at Sacred Heart School. She did enter the order, and she eventually taught at both Sacred Heart and Queen of Angels Schools.

In 1984, during the investigation of Fr. Solanus's life of virtue, Carmella testified before the archdiocesan tribunal in Detroit. She emphasized how he was available for any emergency. In fact, all the sick of Sacred Heart Parish received his special attention. His visits to their homes brought comfort and encouragement, even acceptance of their trials and sufferings. Remarkable cures were believed to have resulted through his prayers and blessings.

Whenever he was not required at the office, Solanus liked to visit homes in the parish. He took a great interest in the ordinary problems of the people. His gentle words brought comfort and encouragement. If his visit was near their time for supper, the folks would persuade him to eat with them. Not wanting to disappoint the family, he would join their meal with engaging simplicity. To all parishioners he was a welcome friend.

During World War I he often visited parish families whose sons were leaving for the armed services. He blessed the young men, prayed for their safety, and assured many that they would return unharmed from battle. After the War, several testified how they had been preserved from certain danger.

His work with the altar boys became another outlet for Solanus's zeal. He tried to instill in them a real spirit of devotion and reverence and was quick to admonish them when they became mischievous or careless. He enjoyed taking them in a group on little excursions to the park, either on foot or via the subway. There would usually be a stop for an ice cream treat. Working with young people helped Solanus remain young at heart.

SOLANUS SAVES THE DAY

Parish activities always engaged his interest. The summer picnics, where he especially enjoyed the hot dogs—with onions—delighted him. On one occasion he offered to prepare a big pot of baked beans for a fall outing. Referring to himself as the Inspector, he wrote about this memorable event:

> A certain monastery...wishing to forestall the financial drain often consequent on Thanksgiving dinners, proclaimed to friends...the staging of a real Boston Baked Beans Dinner...to be just a week ahead of the great turkey Thursday. The Inspector himself was given the privilege of superintending the beans, supposed to be... the highlight of the meal.
>
> Priding himself more or less on the distinction, his first step was to get in touch with the amiable Brother Cook. They decided to put the beans to soak the Sunday night instead of Tuesday before the dinner. They boiled them and had them in the best condition [by] Monday evening. When others sampled them the next morning they seemed even further improved. "Unsurpassable,"

was the word. Three days to wait...seemed long, but we were content—confident—that the delay would not lessen their value and appreciation.

But our pride...was to get a really practical jolt. Thursday finally came and was ideal—could hardly be more promising for a successful affair that night. So wishing to further cooperate with Brother Cook, the Inspector made his way to the monastery kitchen. Brother, too, was in the best of smiles as they met at the kitchen door.

"Oh, Brother Cook!" exclaimed the Inspector, on seeing the previously baked beans, fifty gallons strong, leisurely sitting on the heated back of the stove where they had been since Monday. "That is a bad place for those beans. They should have been in a cool place for keeping." He sampled them.

"Sour," he exclaimed. "Sour," sighed Brother as he tasted them. They gazed vacantly at each other, and both felt stupidly guilty. They both thought of the same baseball phrase, "Three men on base—Casey struck out."

"Wait," said one of them with a gleam of hope. "Saleratus (baking soda) sweetens sour milk if not too far gone. Let us try it on the beans." They boiled a sample quantity, adding a pinch of saleratus. The unintended experiment, with the magic powder coming to the rescue, had made the beans a credit for a king's banquet. Such at least was the general verdict that night.[1]

Another time Solanus was remembered at Sacred Heart Church for "saving the day." The parish challenged the neighboring Queen of Angels Parish to see which one could sell the most tickets for the fundraising drive. Sacred Heart Parish would use the combined proceeds to build a new church. Solanus directed the sale of tickets for Sacred Heart; his classmate, Fr. John O'Donovan, directed it at Queen of Angels.

The day the contest closed, Fr. John and his volunteers were ahead. Suddenly Fr. Solanus remembered that he had another box of ticket stubs in his room. He brought out the box, and when all the stubs were counted, the prize—a new set of vestments—went to Sacred Heart. Solanus was the hero of the day, further endeared to all the hardworking people of Sacred Heart Parish.

REACHING OUT

On occasion Solanus's parochial duties included visiting parishioners employed as servants in the homes of non-Catholics. He showed a special concern for the spiritual welfare of these employers and usually won their esteem and affection.

A noted friend at this time was the famous Anglican convert Paul Francis Wattson. Solanus became acquainted with Paul Francis when his group of Anglican Franciscans entered the Catholic Church. Solanus was present when Fr. Paul was ordained a Catholic priest on June 16, 1910. At Fr. Paul's request, Solanus preached for his friend's first Mass, July 3, 1910, at Graymoor, New York. He kept in touch with Fr. Wattson and his little Society of the Atonement, with a genuine interest.

Solanus's first year in "picturesque Yonkers," as he described it in a letter, was spent in the company of Fr. Stephen Eckert. This saintly Capuchin, a few years his senior, had great zeal for souls, and Solanus admired his work with non-Catholics. When Stephen Eckert was declared Servant of God in 1948, Solanus was called as a witness for his cause of canonization.

Stephen was reassigned to Milwaukee to begin an apostolate among Black people. Solanus continued to reach out to the non-Catholic neighbors of Sacred Heart's parishioners.

Immersed as he was in the work of the Church for the salvation of souls, Solanus yet remained attentive to the times in which he lived. Daily events in the world around him frequently called for prayers of supplication, especially when suffering was involved.

The tragic sinking of the great ocean liner Titanic on the night of April 15, 1912, evoked this short, poignant note:

> Giant steamer, Titanic, bumped against an iceberg, and the pride of naval equipment was buried in a watery grave with [over] 1200 passengers. Nearly 1000 souls were rescued.

Another sad entry of the same year recalls one of his altar boys:

> Dec. 31st. Happy death of altar boy Martin Kennedy, at 3:00 a.m. Had served 93 times during 1911. A dear good boy of eleven years. Jan. 2nd. Buried Martin Kennedy—six altar boys [were] pall-bearers. May he rest in peace.

The page beginning that year of 1912 has this somber note:

> The old year closed with a dreary day—rain, snow, and fog—as though mourning at prospects it had to leave for the new year of trouble and promises of war on all sides and directions.

And this note in a lighter vein: "Fr. Solanus shot [rifle] to scare a dog away from stable and sadly wounded the poor creature."[2]

Such little observations reveal Solanus as a man of feeling, attuned to everyday life.

FAMILY REUNION

Around the time of Solanus's ordination and transfer to New York, his two brothers, John and Tom, began to practice law in Montana. They soon moved further west. Gradually the other brothers and sisters followed them, until all settled in Seattle, Washington, even their aging parents.

Some of the letters written to his sisters and brothers show an interest in and prayerful attention to their joys and sorrows. Through these letters he remained close to the family he loved and who loved him in return.

While Solanus was at Sacred Heart in Yonkers, he had the opportunity to reunite with that fond family when his parents observed their golden wedding anniversary. It was a long train journey from the Atlantic coast to the Pacific, but Solanus experienced great wonder and joy in the panoramic beauty of the vast United States. He joined his brothers Edward and Jim in St. Paul, Minnesota, and they met Maurice in Plains, Montana.

On October 6, 1913, all fourteen of the living Casey children, with spouses, children, and grandchildren, gathered at Immaculate Conception Church in Seattle for the Solemn High Mass of thanksgiving. It was a day of great rejoicing for this close-knit family. The three priest sons celebrated the liturgy. Solanus's notes describe the event:

> October 6th. Parents' Golden Jubilee [with] Solemn High Mass at 9:30. Celebrant, Rev. Maurice Casey of Plains, Deacon, Fr. Solanus of Yonkers, Subdeacon, Rev. Edw. Casey of St. Paul. After Mass a beautiful and poetic program. In evening songs—old and new with original poems and music for the occasion.
>
> October 7th. Mass in Carmelite Convent at 7 a.m. Bade good-bye to parents and friends, hoping to meet in Heaven if never again on earth.[3]

As deacon, Solanus preached. His theme extolled the love and faith that these parents had shared with their children. He poured out his soul in praise and gratitude to the good God for such wonderful parents. These were words that spoke for the whole family.

This was Solanus's last visit with his dear father and mother. Two years later Bernard Casey, Sr. died a peaceful death, surrounded by most of his children, and he was buried in the Franciscan habit of a Tertiary. Ellen Casey Traynor wrote her brother Solanus that "Papa looked just like you." Three years later Ellen Murphy Casey followed her husband after a short battle with pneumonia.

Solanus was not able to travel out West for either funeral, but he was consoled to remember his parents' beautiful lives of faith. He often spoke of their genuine virtues to inspire parents he counseled.

The day after the anniversary celebration Solanus again boarded the train for the long return journey to Yonkers. He wanted to be back in time for the laying of the cornerstone for Sacred Heart's new church—a stone doubly special to Solanus, as it had been made of marble from Ireland. The new church was a splendid edifice in which Solanus and parishioners alike took great pride.

Five

THE SERAPHIC MASS ASSOCIATION

*If our love of God were really genuine, we would quite
naturally love our neighbor as ourselves.*
—FR. SOLANUS

Fr. Solanus's fourteen years of service in Yonkers came to an end after the provincial chapter of July 1918, when he was transferred to the Capuchins' parish of Our Lady of Sorrows in lower Manhattan. His new superior, Fr. Venantius Buessing, appointed him sacristan and made him director of the Young Ladies' Sodality. The young women later remembered him for the eloquent and fervent homilies that he gave for their instruction.

While Solanus did not have the formal "patents" for preaching, he did give little homilies or "fervorinos" with great unction at devotions and Sunday liturgies. About fourteen of these simple exhortations are preserved among his collected writings. They are inspiring exhortations to love God and one's neighbor. Based mainly on the Scripture readings for the day, they give us an insight into Solanus's heart and mind.

The following provincial chapter, three years later, transferred Solanus to the Capuchins' parish of Our Lady of Angels in Harlem, New York. Once again he accepted the duties of porter at the monastery. Before long he was as busy and as much in demand among the people in Harlem as he had been during the years in Yonkers.

HELP FOR THE MISSIONS

Here his work seems to have given new impetus to the Seraphic Mass Association (or SMA, as it came to be called). This work was founded in Switzerland at the beginning of the century as a means of support for the foreign missions under the care of Capuchins. People who made a small offering for the missions and enrolled their names in the Seraphic Mass Association would share in the benefits of the many Masses celebrated in Capuchin communities around the world.

Solanus felt that here was a way for people to help the missions and at the same time obtain God's help for their own needs. He also saw it as a wonderful means of promoting devotion to and appreciation for the Holy Sacrifice of the Mass.

When people came to him asking God's help and blessing in sickness or trials, he always suggested that they "do something to please the Dear Lord." He would often get them to promise more frequent attendance at Holy Mass and reception of Holy Communion. He would also suggest they make an offering for enrollment in the association.

The people at Our Lady of Angels soon noticed that when Fr. Solanus enrolled a person in the Seraphic Mass Association, wonderful results and even cures were the outcome. They would go back to him with profuse thanks, but he always attributed the favors to the merits of the Holy Mass and urged them to give all thanks to God.

This assignment at Our Lady of Angels meant a new and more pastoral role for Solanus. More and more people now sought him out as a spiritual counselor and advocate. He felt it a duty to be available for all in need, and by promoting the Seraphic Mass Association he could be a missionary, too. For the rest of his life this would be his main apostolate. From this time on, aid for the Capuchin missions continued to grow noticeably, a work that still goes on today under the name of the Capuchin Mission Association.

FR. SOLANUS'S NOTEBOOKS

This very effective apostolate of Solanus soon came to the notice of his provincial, Fr. Benno Aichinger. During the provincial visitation in 1923, at Our Lady of Angels Friary, Fr. Benno asked Fr. Solanus and the other friars about the remarkable favors being attributed to enrollment in the Seraphic Mass Association. Fr. Benno thought it would be important to have some record of these events, so he ordered Solanus to keep a log of the answers to prayer. So began Solanus's famous "Notebooks of Favors Reported."

With his customary enthusiasm, Solanus began immediately to enter notes in a large ten-by-twelve-inch ledger:

> **Nov. 8, 1923.** Today [the Provincial] Visitation closed. Fr. Provincial wishes notes to be made of special favors reported as through the Seraphic Mass Association.
>
> Deo Gratias! This p.m. Margaret Quinn, who enrolled her neighbor against drink and consequent anger on Oct. 26, as also her sister from Philadelphia, against severe inflammatory rheumatism, reports wonderful improvement in former and a letter this a.m. from her sister—"Thank God and the good prayer society, I'm feeling fine."

> **Jan. 8, 1924.** Mrs. Sawler enrolled May 3, 1923—given three days to live with pneumonia—family doctor gave her three hours— report [today] recovered completely.

> **Jan. 14.** Jennie McCabe promised a year ago to put Poor Souls in SMA if serious heart failure improved. Doctor surprised that she

lived. Today in evident health, gave five perpetual memberships for Poor Souls.

Feb. 2. Patrick Hardiman enrolled crippled mother on Jan. 14. Feb. 2 reports—Jan. 20, no pain—now [she] goes to holy Mass...goes shopping as twenty years ago.

Feb. 25. Conversion after 29 years. Mary Galbally, who enrolled her father perpetually on Nov. 6, reports this evening—overjoyed at result—"Papa went to confession and holy communion this morning for first time in 49 years." She had heard on Nov. 4 of a conversion as through SMA after 35 years and determined to try the same for her loved father. She would wish now to proclaim from the mountaintops the goodness of God as through same SMA.

March 28. Cured from gangrene diabetes. Patrick McCue enrolled for one year Feb. 9, by fellow motorman—reported today entirely cured of both [gangrene and diabetes], and working every day. Doctors baffled![1]

So the notes go on. Some are very short, almost cryptic, without details or final results, but all have a note of hope for God's help. The following very interesting report was noted in 1925 after Fr. Solanus went to Detroit:

March 12, 1925. Big Company Enrolled. Chevrolet—Thursday Feb. 12, 8 p.m. "Father, I don't know what to do," said John McKenna, a friend and zealous promoter of Seraphic Mass Association. "I have not had a full day in two weeks, and today I got less than two hours." A short pause and McKenna resumes, as by inspiration: "Father, put the company in the Mass Association." I smiled a moment—sure it was an introduction of something new— then agreed, knowing it must bring a blessing of some kind. The Chevrolet Company is enrolled for a year, at the time producing

65-70 machines per hour when running rightly. Feb. 13, Company is reported to have orders for 45,000 machines in 30 days. March 12—exactly four weeks later—300 per hour was [the] output.[2]

Fr. Solanus wrote in this first notebook almost daily. The last entry was on April 18, 1932:

Pneumonia—Mrs. Cosgain—enrolled last Thursday at 4 p.m. hopelessly sick with pneumonia—emphysema and in a coma. Got well immediately and went for a ride Saturday.[3]

He would eventually fill more than seven notebooks with over six thousand entries, up to the year 1956. To him these favors were a sign of the goodness and mercy of God's love for his people. In no way were they tributes to himself but only to the all-good God.

LOVING THE WORLD

Solanus's three years at the friary in Harlem were filled with many varied activities. His Irish roots made him a natural advocate in the cause for justice at this time in his parents' homeland. Ireland's struggle for freedom from the British yoke touched him deeply. On several occasions he was invited to address rallies of some of the Irish societies in New York City, and he even wrote a letter to the editor of the local newspaper calling for justice for the people of Ireland in their fight for home rule.

Another small notebook, discovered in the provincial archives only in 1990, makes reference to this more public activity. Solanus expressed some concern that he was acting correctly in these appearances and appeals for justice. He made a point of discussing the issue with Cardinal Hayes, archbishop of New York. He asked His Eminence about speaking at the convention of the A.A.R.I.R. (American Association for Recognition of the Irish Republic).

"Am I doing right?"

Cardinal Hayes replied, "It's all right, Father. Encourage the people and console them in every way you can."

Notes in the same journal reveal his pastoral concern for another band of suffering humanity, the prisoners at a nearby Harlem prison. These prisoners were mostly poor Black men. They were attended only occasionally with a short service or sermon.

Solanus had a real sensitivity to all human suffering, and his heart went out to these neglected prisoners. From 1922 to 1924 he tried to give them the benefits of a regular Sunday Mass. He even took a more personal approach, noting once that he was able to provide "Xmas cards for all." He also noted "having given the pledge" (a promise not to drink for a period of time) and "sharing newspapers with them."

PERSONAL TRIALS

During these years at Our Lady of Angels, Solanus had to endure certain physical sufferings himself. It seems that in 1921 some sort of gangrenous infection brought him close to death.

He wrote to his sister Margaret LeDoux from the hospital: "I had been in agony for at least forty hours, though no one else seemed to know it, and while I tried to thank God for it all, my principal prayer—at least a thousand times repeated—was 'God, help us.'"

Another patient's urgent case of appendicitis delayed his own operation. While waiting, he wrote, his pain lessened a bit, yet he continued to pray, "God, help us," and sometimes added, "*Deo gratias.*" After describing the strange sensation of being anesthetized, he went on:

> Life and light were going by fast when beautiful bells began to ring.... A voice gently and piously reminded: "There's the Angelus." Oh, how sweet was that music to my soul and the announcement,

how confidence inspiring! Then I realized that consciousness had come to the very end. The description of Mother's beautiful death three years ago at the second ringing of the Angelus flashed on my memory, and my heart was able to respond: "Behold, be it done to me according to Your holy will."[4]

The doctor was able to cut away the infected tissue. It healed quickly, so Solanus could return home within a few days. His sentiments of gratitude for God's help in this ordeal far outweighed the memories of the pain endured.

He would experience hospitals several times in later life. When referring to these occasions, he always had a note of thanksgiving for being able to share in the sufferings of Jesus. His own sufferings also gave him an increased appreciation for the pain and sufferings of others.

The next provincial chapter made changes in personnel again. This time Fr. Solanus was transferred to the headquarters of the province, St. Bonaventure Monastery in Detroit, to give assistance to the porter there. With just a few days' notice he left Harlem, arriving in Detroit on the first day of August 1924. This vast metropolis would now benefit from the holy man's compassion and dedication.

Six

MINISTRY IN DETROIT

Our lot has been cast among the simple lives of the poor.
—FR. SOLANUS

The next twenty-one years were a time of total dedication to serving the sick and the poor in the burgeoning city of the Midwest, Detroit, Michigan. Sent by the superiors to be the assistant to Br. Francis Spruck, monastery porter for over twenty-five years, Solanus soon became the one friar whom everybody wanted to see. Within weeks the short lists of people enrolled in the Seraphic Mass Association noticeably increased to several pages of names for each day, and with a good increase of donations for the missions. Poor Br. Francis, who was provincial tailor and porter at the same time, had hoped that the new porter would lessen his work at the office. Now, as Solanus became more and more known, the doorbell rang constantly. The friars finally put a sign over the bell, "WALK IN."

The fame of Solanus spread by word of mouth all over the city. When people were sick or in difficulty, the word was, "Go see Father Solanus." He was everybody's friend, and like a good friend he was always available.

On a typical day at the monastery office, all the chairs lined up around the room would be occupied. People patiently waited a turn to speak with

Solanus, who sat at a plain desk in the center of the room. Sometimes he would be interrupted by the telephone on his desk. He would turn his attention to the caller, always with patience and equanimity.

Every visitor was important to Solanus. He never hurried anyone. With complete attention he patiently listened to each tale of concern for a sick child or parent or friend. Gently he would speak of God's love and how God turns trials to blessings. He would try to share his own deep faith and trust in God with the person before him.

In one of his letters he expresses the importance of faith: "Humanity's sad weakness—lack of faith, and consequently, want of confidence in God."

In another letter he writes:

> There is such a thing as getting "a taste of heaven" in this world, as we see in the lives of the saints. But it is up to each of us to strive for—inasmuch as our virtue of hope is inspired by faith in God and strengthened—sweetened—in confidence of His great merciful goodness.[1]

Solanus's strong faith would inspire people. He would help them grow in faith so that they could pray in faith. And their prayers would be answered.

FAVORS REPORTED

Solanus's notebooks are full of remarkable favors granted to people after being enrolled in the Seraphic Mass Association. There are notes about suicides averted and fallen-away Catholics returned to the sacraments—all kinds of mental, physical, and spiritual healings. Many are the added comments—"*Deo gratias*" or "Thanks be to God"—after a cure or a prayer was answered.

Solanus recognized the alcohol problem as a sickness to be cured by more than just willpower. He knew the need for the help of a "Higher

Power" long before the "Twelve Steps" of Alcoholics Anonymous were widely known. His encouragement and prayers saved many a life enslaved by the bottle.

James Derum, Fr. Solanus's first biographer, interviewed a man who told of his cure from alcoholism. His life seemed miserable and hopeless. He prayed for strength and tried to quit but felt it was impossible. One Sunday afternoon he came to the monastery. Fr. Solanus saw him to a private room, then left him to say good-bye to the couple at his desk.

Solanus went back in, sat down, and let the man talk. Several times Br. Francis interrupted him to say that others were waiting. Solanus would say, "Ask them to wait a little longer." He continued to listen patiently to the man.

Finally Solanus asked, "When did you get over your sickness?" The man was surprised that Solanus called it a sickness. The assumption that he was cured was even more astounding.

"You mean my drunk, Father?" the man asked. Solanus laughed—a gentle, encouraging kind of laugh—and reassured him of God's grace and help. He then blessed him. The man went out with a great sense of freedom and never took a drink again.

LET THE CHILDREN COME

Coming from a large family of sixteen children with parents who truly loved them, Solanus inherited a love for children that was God-centered. He expressed it tenderly in a letter to his niece Helena Wilhite:

> To raise children for God and society is so manifestly pleasing to God—and this, whether they [are] by natural generation or by adoption (seemingly quite a matter of indifference to Him), that He has given a specially beautiful coloring to the love of those whose privilege it is to have become earnest, faithful parents.[2]

This love for children made Fr. Solanus their special intercessor. When the dread polio epidemic struck in the thirties, many who called on his prayers were wonderfully restored to health, to the surprise of their doctors. One case, that of twelve-year-old Charles Rogers, was described vividly by his sister when she was interviewed a few years ago. Young Charles was getting stiff in the neck and limbs. The doctor, a well-known specialist, came to the house to examine him. He wanted to get the boy to the hospital right away, but his father waited. He asked one of his workers to see Fr. Solanus and ask for his prayers. Fr. Solanus enrolled Charles in the Mass Association and told his father, "Don't worry. The boy will be all right tomorrow."

During the night Charles startled his parents by walking downstairs. They put him back to bed and called his doctor immediately. When the doctor came, he tested the strength in the boy's arms and legs, then told him to walk.

The doctor was completely surprised. He had never seen anything like this before. He told Mr. Rogers, "You did more than pray; this is a miracle!" Medical men don't usually use that term.

There were couples who were praying for children but had such difficulties conceiving that they almost despaired. They found that Solanus's prayers were very effective in obtaining the blessings of children. Even to this day so many people have reported how Solanus's prayers have helped achieve and maintain pregnancies that he might be considered a special intercessor for such requests.

Prophetic Gifts

It seems that there were times when Solanus had the gift of prophecy. A young woman came to ask his prayers because she wanted to become a nun.

"No," he told her, "you will marry a young man, and he will become a policeman, and you will have several children." Some years after Solanus's death, this woman reported that she indeed had married a soldier who became a policeman, and they had eight children.

One evening a lady came into the office. She had just come from seeing her husband in the hospital. She asked Solanus's prayers and requested that he telephone her husband and give him some words of comfort.

Solanus called the man's room and told him that his wife was in the office and had asked for prayers for his recovery. After a few words of encouragement he said to the man, "Now, John, I will be praying for you this evening. I am going to pray for a happy death."

It was not what the man or his wife expected to hear, but Solanus was able to prepare them to accept God's plan. The following day the man died a happy, peaceful death, and his wife and family found peace also.

SOUP AND BREAD

Each day was filled with a constant dedication to the needs of people. The spiritual welfare of all was, of course, Solanus's primary concern, but material needs also could prompt his willing service.

Capuchin friaries have always been a haven for the poor, and St. Bonaventure's was well known in Detroit as a place where people could find help. When the Great Depression hit Detroit after the stock market crash of 1929, long lines of unemployed men gathered at the monastery office looking for food.

Fr. Solanus could not turn anyone away, so he prevailed upon the brother cook to prepare extra soup. He and Br. Francis would give each hungry visitor a steaming bowl of thick soup with some bread. This went on for a few weeks until the crowd became too great for them to handle. At that point the director of the Third Order Franciscans came to the rescue.

Fr. Herman Buss, together with the Third Order men and women, volunteered to move the operation to their meeting hall, which was attached to St. Bonaventure Church. Solanus continued to urge many of his friends to offer donations in support of this work of charity. The dedicated Secular Franciscans helped in the kitchen and picked up donations of bread from city bakeries. They were able to provide as many as a thousand meals a day for Detroit's poor.

The hall became one of the first "soup kitchens" in the city, a work of charity that has continued uninterrupted to this day. At two facilities near St. Bonaventure Monastery, the Capuchins are presently serving around two thousand meals daily to Detroit's needy. This generous work is supported solely by the good and generous people of the metropolitan area, many of them inspired by the example of Solanus Casey.

Seven

"DEO GRATIAS"

*How little it is possible for [us] poor mortals to appreciate,
as we ought, or to be properly grateful to God
and our benefactors.*
—FR. SOLANUS

Fr. Solanus's fame won for the monastery and the soup kitchen a generous band of benefactors among Catholics, and among people of other faiths as well. He was quick to recognize that genuine gratitude would insure their support. "Thanks be to God" was the prayer most often on his lips, coming directly from his heart.

Always filled with a true sense of gratitude himself, first to God and then to the benefactors, he tried to lead others to this attitude.

In 1937 he was invited to deliver a little "radio address" at the time of a benefit party arranged for the soup kitchen. The following is the bulk of his talk, an example of the gratitude and appreciation that he felt:

> Good afternoon, my brethren:
> An opportunity was offered to me today to speak to you on the radio. The occasion is the benefit party which some of our friends have arranged for us....We have always known that many of you

have been our friends, but since the preparations for this beautiful party have been in progress, we are convinced of it. From all parts of the city men and women came to us asking how they might help. We Capuchins are told that the city of Detroit wishes to show itself grateful for the help we have given during the days of the Depression. We admit that we have tried to be of service to the poorest of the poor, but must add that it was a simple duty.

St. Francis, our holy founder, impressed it upon his brethren that they must labor for their daily bread. And he added, "Should the wages of our work be not given us, then shall we have recourse to the table of the Lord asking alms from door to door."

Our lot has been cast among the simple lives of the poor, and our object is to give them spiritual aid and, if possible, material help as well. When speaking of those days of the Depression, we cannot forget that our work in relieving the misery of poverty was made possible only by the willing cooperation of such people as bakers who supplied bread, the farmers who gave us vegetables, and our numerous friends who made donations from their fairly empty purses.

It is to these generous souls that we want to pay tribute today. May the all-bountiful God, who leaves no glass of water offered in His name to pass unrewarded, recompense the generosity of our friends with true happiness—the peace of the soul. Our gratitude extends to them and to all who are helping to make this benefit a success. We are deeply appreciative of all [that] you have done for us, and in return, assure you that you are remembered in all the prayers and good works of our numerous Capuchin brethren.

It is our sincere hope that this harmony of interest and action may never be broken. Our community is at the service of those who may require it. And as long as we are among you...we will have the needs of the poor at heart and will relieve their misery as best we can. Once more, let me thank you, one and all, in the name of our Capuchin community. May mutual appreciation be the soul of our relationship in the future, as this party...seems to prove it has been in the past. God bless you all.[1]

AN ATTITUDE OF GRATITUDE

Many were the occasions, when speaking with the friars or other people, that Solanus would extol the importance and necessity of gratitude. His letters express this theme over and over. He calls gratitude "the first sign of a thinking, rational creature." Another simple expression of gratitude is found in a short poem that he wrote:

> God made me to know Him.
>   O! what a blessed aim!
> To love Him and serve Him
>   Sure rests in the same.
> It's heaven begun
>   For the grateful on earth.
> To treasure aright—
>   Highest Heaven, its worth.[2]

To some people asking for God's help in their needs, he would suggest that they "thank God ahead of time." This might seem a bold idea, sort of "putting God on the spot," as he explained to one of the brothers, but certainly a great leap of faith.

While Solanus could not get personally involved in the daily work of the soup kitchen, he did keep close to it by urging others to support it, especially when he came into contact with people of means. He considered this charity toward the poor one of the best ways to thank God and obtain heavenly favors. His own fervent prayers on behalf of the poor sometimes obtained remarkable results.

One day Fr. Herman sent word over to Fr. Solanus that they were running out of bread. Solanus left his desk and hurried over to the soup kitchen. He asked the people standing around waiting for the meal to join him in praying the Our Father.

As they finished the prayer there was a knock at the door. A man came in with a large basket of bread and said that he had a truck full of loaves outside. After all the bread was brought in and piled up, the man looked at the pile in amazement and said, "That's more than the truck could hold."

SUNDAYS AT ST. PAUL'S

During this time Fr. Solanus became engaged in some parish work. Early in 1935 Fr. Michael Cefai, pastor of St. Paul's Maltese Church near downtown Detroit, came to the monastery seeking a priest to help with Sunday Masses. Fr. Marion Reossler, the superior, had just told Fr. Cefai that no one was available. Solanus walked by at the moment, and Fr. Cefai said, "How about Fr. Solanus?"

"Well," said Fr. Marion, "he doesn't usually help in parishes because he does not hear confessions." Fr. Cefai replied that he would need him only for the Sunday Mass. Solanus spoke up then and told Fr. Marion that he would be willing to go.

For the next several years one of St. Paul's ushers would pick up Fr. Solanus and drive him to the church for Sunday Mass. Fr. Cefai usually gave the homily in Maltese, but sometimes he allowed Solanus to preach. His brief homilies were mainly simple admonitions to the people to have more faith and trust in God.

The people came to revere Fr. Solanus as a holy priest, and they loved to attend his Mass. After Mass they would stop to speak with him about their problems and concerns. He promised his prayers for them but also urged them to pray. He encouraged them to grow in faith and confidence in the "Dear Lord."

Fr. Cefai's father, mother, and two sisters lived in the rectory and worked for the parish. They usually had Fr. Solanus stay for dinner after his Mass, as he was very fond of their spaghetti. Fr. Cefai and his whole family loved Solanus for his kindness and virtue and sought his prayers for their needs, too.

One time Fr. Cefai misplaced his keys for the church and tabernacle. He searched his pockets and everywhere in the house but did not find them. When Fr. Solanus arrived for Mass, Fr. Cefai told him of the lost keys and his desperation.

"Look in your right-hand pocket," Solanus said. Even though Fr. Cefai had gone through his pockets several times, now the keys were there.

Another time the pastor's father had spent a sleepless night in great pain. When Solanus arrived and learned of Mr. Cefai's suffering, he immediately went in to talk to him. Solanus gently urged him to offer up his pain for sinners. Within a short time the pain ceased, to Mr. Cefai's surprise and relief.

THE MYSTICAL CITY OF GOD

Here at St. Paul's, Solanus unwittingly became involved in something of a controversy. In 1904 or 1905 he had discovered the four-volume work *The Mystical City of God* by a Spanish nun, Venerable Mary of Agreda. This inspiring life of Our Blessed Mother impressed him deeply, and he immediately began to study it. Years later he wrote the following praise of this work on the flyleaf of Volume Three of a set that he used:

> Shortly after my ordination to the holy priesthood I heard of a "Life of the Blessed Virgin." I was skeptical. Who could think of presuming to write the life of the Blessed Virgin these days? So I figured, erroneously taking it as generally understood that it had never, as yet, been written. However, I was determined to see if it possibly might be more than a compilation of favors, etc., like

the "Glories of Mary," which my father used to peddle in the wintertime....

We found an abridged copy of *The Mystical City of God*. What a revelation! What a treasure! From that first perusal of the simple but masterly introduction by the humble secretary—the actual writer—my conviction has grown that the same *Mystical City of God*, of whose four volumes this present is the third, is not only a genuine "life" of the same, our Blessed Mother Mary, but, having studied it for more than forty years and on my knees having prayed the whole four volumes, I am convinced that the work has been rightly referred to as the most opportune and authentic autobiography of the Blessed Virgin herself, the Queen of all creation and chosen by the Divine Creator Himself to be His own Spouse and Mother. Glory be to God![3]

Together with the Holy Scriptures, this life of Mary became Solanus's favorite study. Above all, he tried to imitate the sublime virtues of Mary, especially her humility and conformity to God's will, as they were portrayed in these volumes. He sometimes recommended the reading of this work to others who he felt might find profit for their spiritual life.

Some of these people organized a little group devoted to the study of *The Mystical City of God*. Led by a friend of Solanus who was promoting the sale of the work, they began to attend Solanus's Mass at St. Paul's. Eventually they asked to gather in the church basement to discuss the book. The pastor gave his consent but insisted that Fr. Solanus be present with them.

This went fine for a few months, until Solanus became ill and was hospitalized. The leader of the group had great affection for Fr. Solanus but was an aggressive sort of individual. While Solanus was in the hospital, this man continued to gather the devotees at St. Paul's without consulting Solanus or Fr. Cefai. During one of their meetings he managed to telephone Solanus's hospital room, and he asked him to transmit a greeting and blessing to the assembled group.

Fr. Cefai became quite upset at this unorthodox activity. He complained to Solanus and the superior at St. Bonaventure's, and he withdrew his permission to hold the meetings at St. Paul's.

The matter resulted in a painful situation for Solanus. He thought that these devotees were acting in good faith. The superior, however, felt they were imposing on Fr. Solanus's zeal for their own ends.

Eventually the superior forbade Solanus to have any more dealings with this group or their leader. Solanus felt that his friends had been misunderstood, but in a spirit of obedience, he faithfully submitted to the superior's ban.

VOCATIONAL COUNSELING

People sometimes asked Solanus for his prayers and direction concerning a vocation to the religious life or the priesthood. One day six or seven young ladies, postulants for the Felician Sisters in Detroit, approached him.

Their problem was that they wanted to enter the Felician novitiate, but their superior had decided that they must wait until there was a group of twelve. Solanus heard their request and then told them that they would indeed be invested as novices within the year. Soon after, more young women applied as postulants, and before the end of the year twelve novices were invested.

Another young lady, whose uncle was one of Solanus's regular drivers, experienced his prayer and persistence for her vocation. She often accompanied her uncle while driving Fr. Solanus on his visits to the sick. A few times, when her uncle was not able to get away from his work to drive Solanus, she drove for him.

When the woman's older sister entered the Immaculate Heart Sisters in Monroe, Michigan, Solanus suggested that she might have a vocation also. The thought of a religious vocation had occurred to her, but she was inclined to question the idea. She was a talented young woman and not really inclined to religious life.

She asked Solanus one day, "Do you think I have a vocation?"

He answered, "Well, God does queer things." Then he asked her, "You don't want to be a sister, do you?" When she said, "No, I don't want to," he replied, "Then why are you thinking about it?"

Solanus would bring the conversation on the subject so far and then change to something else. Finally, by the grace of God and Solanus's encouragement, the woman's resistance wore down. She too joined the Sisters of the Immaculate Heart of Mary. After her initial training and studies, she went on to serve her order in many responsible positions.

A few years ago a priest of the Detroit archdiocese related his experience to a group of Father Solanus Guild members. While a young student at Detroit's Sacred Heart Seminary, he began to have stomach problems. He feared that he would have to give up his studies. His mother suggested that they call on Fr. Solanus.

When they came to the monastery office, the young man asked Solanus if he should become a priest. He blessed the young man and told him not to worry. "You will be a priest," he said, "and serve the Church for a long time." He is now retired after fifty years in the priesthood and remains ever grateful for Fr. Solanus's intercession.

I, too, feel that Fr. Solanus's prayers and blessing helped me realize my vocation to the Capuchin Brothers. I am one of the fruits of his Detroit ministry. I was further blessed to come into a unique relationship with him, in which I could see for myself his holiness and dedication.

Eight

Witnesses to Holiness

If we are interested in saving our souls, we must have an interest in our sisters and brothers.
—Fr. Solanus

I came to know Fr. Solanus in 1938. I had spoken to my parish priest about an interest in the Franciscan Order, and he advised me to speak to Fr. Solanus at St. Bonaventure Monastery. After a short talk he suggested that I join the Junior Third Order. This was a very active group of young people involved at St. Bonaventure's.

During the following year I began serving at the early Masses at the monastery and came to know the friars well. The hidden life of service of the brothers appealed to me, and within the year I became a candidate and entered the novitiate, located at that time at St. Bonaventure's.

In the community I enjoyed the company of many holy friars but especially that of Fr. Solanus. To serve his Mass was a special experience of holy joy for me and is a cherished memory today.

Healing Prayer

This was during the years when Solanus was at the height of his fame as an extraordinarily holy man. He was known for the wonders he obtained by prayer for many of the sick and for troubled souls around Detroit and beyond.

In May of 1941, after I made profession as a Capuchin brother, my first assignment was to work in the monastery office with Solanus. Because so many people were coming day after day to see him, it was necessary to have one of the brothers at the office to take care of those who were not waiting to see him. Br. Francis Spruck, who had been porter at St. Bonaventure's for almost fifty years, was aging and failing in health. The superior wanted to give him some relief, so he assigned me to take his place at the desk for a few hours a day.

This became for me a great opportunity to observe the attention and care Fr. Solanus gave to all the suffering people who came to him. While I never witnessed any sudden or dramatic cures, I was privileged to observe many instances that convince me today of his genuine holiness.

One remarkable example happened to Br. Daniel Brady, a novice. He had a serious tooth condition that required an operation on the bone. Fearful for the outcome, Daniel asked Solanus to bless his tooth before he went to the dentist.

That afternoon a friend brought Solanus a little box with three ice cream cones. As people were waiting to see him, Solanus just set the box inside his desk.

Later, when all the visitors were gone, Br. Daniel walked into the office all smiles. He told Solanus that the dentist found the tooth in sound condition! There was no need for an operation.

"Thanks be to God," Solanus said. Then he added, "That calls for a celebration." Reaching down into his desk, he brought out the box of ice cream cones. They had not melted, and the three of us enjoyed the treats.

Another striking instance of Solanus's gift of healing is recounted by Fr. Marion Roessler, Solanus's superior in the 1930s:

The list of alleged cures is so long that to my mind none of our friars ever took the trouble to keep a record of them. One case remains vivid in my mind. It concerns…a crippled child who had not walked in years.

The child was held on the lap of an adult. Fr. Solanus enrolled the child in the Seraphic Mass Association and blessed the child. He then told the child to walk over to his desk. (They were sitting at some distance from him.)

The child immediately got on his feet and walked over to Fr. Solanus. The parents were almost hysterical and wild with joy. Another time a woman told me that after her marriage, when she was finally bearing a child, the doctor had told her that it was impossible for her to deliver the child. Either she or the child would die. I asked Fr. Solanus to bless her, and she had a safe delivery.[1]

STILL THE HUMBLE PORTER

Fr. Marion also described Solanus's pastoral care for the sick and his practice of simplicity and obedience:

Fr. Solanus conducted the weekly service at our monastery chapel, the blessing of the sick with the relic of the True Cross.

His simple discourses in connection with this weekly devotion consisted in admonishing the people to strive to come closer to God through frequent reception of the sacraments, prayer, and conformity to God's Holy Will in all the events of their lives. He insisted that penance was very necessary to make up for sin, and for the salvation of souls....

Fr. Solanus possessed the biblical simplicity of the dove, without having the cunning of the serpent. In his deep Irish faith, his Catholic practice was that of an innocent child. His religious obedience was naturally linked to holy simplicity, even as St. Francis linked these two virtues. His humility made it easy for him to realize his limited abilities in theory and practice. Thus, he was always most obedient and docile in his dealings with his superiors.[2]

The daily stream of people coming to see Solanus was at times exhausting. After his later move to Brooklyn, he wrote to encourage me in my duty as porter: "Even though fraught with dangers, it [the duty of porter] has many advantages, if only we be of good will, and cooperate with the graces never failing on God's part and [that of] our Blessed Mother." Then he added: "Sometimes of course it becomes monotonous and extremely boring, till one is nearly collapsing."[3]

From this I could see how difficult the porter's work was for him at times. I recall moments when he seemed quite tired. He might ask people at the desk to wait there for a few minutes. He would then go back into one of the small private offices for five or ten minutes and return somewhat refreshed. I went in one time and discovered that he had lain on the floor with a book under his head for a little catnap.

Among my duties at the desk was answering most of the mail sent to Solanus. The crush of people waiting to see him every day allowed him almost no time for correspondence. A few of the most pathetic letters were given him, but even these might wait for days before he could find time for a reply.

Simple Faith

As I look back now, I realize how fortunate I was to be in the presence of Fr. Solanus. I could see the patience and compassion with which he greeted each person who came seeking help for body or soul.

There were two chairs in front of his desk, and he would invite visitors to sit down, putting them at ease. After listening to each one's story of sickness or pain, he would speak gently of God and God's great mercy and goodness, sharing his own faith and trust. In this way he would spark the flame of faith and hope in the other person, and then wonderful graces and cures would come about.

Usually Solanus spoke very quietly, but if he needed to emphasize a point his voice might be heard around the room. I remember a time when he exclaimed very distinctly to a worried person, "Don't be anxious about anything!"

Children always received special attention. Ear infections and mastoid conditions were common in those days without antibiotics, and we have many reports of these being cured.

Solanus kept candy in the desk drawer and would offer the children a piece to win their confidence. One day a worried mother brought in her little girl, who had diabetes. She asked Fr. Solanus's prayers for the child, and right away he assured her that she would recover. The mother was aghast when he offered the girl a little piece of candy. It did not hurt the child, and a few days later the mother reported that the diabetes had disappeared.

Other times Fr. Solanus seemed to know if a cure would not come about. A little girl, very seriously sick, was brought in by her parents one evening. They told Solanus about her grave illness, asking prayers for her recovery. He listened quietly and then gently said to them, "You know, the Dear Lord wants little angels for saints, too." And with that he kindly disposed them to accept the child's approaching death with peaceful resignation.

He usually urged people to be grateful to God for all things, even sufferings. On one occasion he said, "When Jesus sends crosses and trials into our life, He is inviting us to help Him save the world."

His counsel often included a plea for more frequent reception of the sacraments. Devotion to the Holy Sacrifice of the Mass and the holy rosary of Our Lady he generally suggested, devotions that he practiced with great fervor himself.

With the promise of his prayers and a little card attesting to enrollment in the Seraphic Mass Association, Solanus would then offer a blessing. Standing—a tall, thin, almost gaunt figure—he would place his hands with their crooked arthritic fingers on the head of the person and softly pray. Sometimes he might playfully tap the person on the head or cheek. A bright smile and twinkling blue eyes gave sparkle to the warm friendly gaze that made everyone feel he was a good friend. One day in 1935, some friends came from Windsor, Ontario, bringing Br. André Bessette of Montreal (now Saint) to meet Solanus. After a short conversation, Br. André knelt down and asked Fr. Solanus for his blessing. Solanus stood up and blessed André, and then Solanus knelt down and asked André for his blessing.

A young priest of the Detroit archdiocese used to stop in regularly just to ask Solanus for his blessing. Solanus would graciously comply, and then he would kneel and ask Father for his blessing. I think this gave a powerful example of humility to the people waiting in the office.

Many people came to see him regularly, bringing their friends or dear ones who were in need of healing. Thus his fame spread from one person to another, until his name was a household word all around Detroit. People knew that if he prayed for them, things would turn out for the better.

LIVING IN GOD'S PRESENCE

The other friars in the monastery took Solanus more or less for granted. He participated in all the community exercises with no preferential treatment. He took a lot of kidding for being late for meals (because he was detained at the office) and for his squeaky violin playing. Some friars jokingly imitated his high-pitched voice. Solanus took all these things in good humor, without any offense.

Solanus usually attended the friars' recreation period after the noon meal. Billiards was one of their usual games, and Solanus was a skilled player. Most of the time his game would be interrupted because of a call to the office. He seemed to expect this, and he did not let interruptions disturb his composure. He very readily returned to his desk and gave his attention to the person waiting for him.

We all knew he was a man of great prayer. We could see his fervor and devotion while celebrating Mass and while assisting at the daily prayers of the community. Often he could be seen in the chapel, late at night or early in the morning. He would kneel before the Blessed Sacrament, deep in prayer for all those who came to him.

Little did we realize the wonderful favors he obtained for people through his prayer and blessing. The bulk of these became known only after his death in 1957, when people began to relate how they had received graces and healing after visiting him.

There is no doubt that Solanus lived constantly in the presence of God. This seemed natural to him. He said once, "We are continually immersed in God's merciful grace, like the air that permeates us." His conversations turned naturally to God; he spoke always of God's grace and goodness and mercy.

People have said that after speaking with Solanus they felt a great weight fall from their shoulders. His advice seemed so simple, yet invariably it went right to the point. He seemed to inspire people to greater confidence and trust.

I remember a particular example of his unselfish dedication. He had been battling a cold for several days, so one quiet evening when all the visitors had left, I suggested that he get away from the office early for some extra rest. He was just walking out when a young couple came in. They saw him and called out, "Father Solanus!" He turned back to his desk and sat down to talk to them.

Later, after ten o'clock, I returned to lock up and found him still there. The two were just leaving, and their smiling faces indicated that Solanus had indeed helped them. When they were gone, I remarked to Solanus, "It's too bad you didn't leave a little quicker and get that rest." He answered gently, "Well, when Jesus was about to fall the second time on the way to Calvary, He stopped to console the weeping women."

SAVING SOULS

Solanus could meet people where they were in their spiritual life and draw them closer to God. When non-Catholics came for help, he respected their position and faith. Certainly "ahead of his time," he was able to reach out to people of other faiths in a simple, friendly way long before Catholics discovered ecumenism. Yet he sometimes might suggest gently that they investigate the claims of the "Mother Church."

"Perhaps you are more Catholic than you think you are," he would say with that little twinkle in his eye and a warm smile. Always grateful for his own Catholic faith, he respected others for whatever faith they had, and he counted several ministers and rabbis as sincere friends. At the same time, his own example of faith inspired many people to enter the Catholic fold.

A gentleman who took delight in driving Solanus to visit sick people was a confirmed Mason with no church affiliation. After many conversations while driving, this man was drawn to take instructions and become a Catholic. He did not let on to his Catholic family that he had been baptized.

At midnight Mass on Christmas Eve, when his wife and children walked up to receive Holy Communion, he surprised them by following them to the altar rail. His startled wife wept for joy when she learned that Fr. Solanus had brought him to the grace of baptism. Many stories like this testify to Solanus's missionary zeal.

James Derum, in his biography of Solanus Casey, tells of a young man who came with two friends to ask Solanus for prayers for his sick father.

"My father is a very good Catholic," the young man began.

"Yes, he is, but you are not," Solanus said very bluntly. The young man blushed.

"Oh, Father," his friends objected, "we know Michael goes to Mass every Sunday."

"He has not been going to Mass and has not been to the sacraments in the last five years," Solanus told them.

The young man admitted this was true, and then he fervently promised that he would return to the sacraments at once. Solanus encouraged him to be faithful. He gave his blessing with an assurance that the young man's father would recover.

Striving for Perfection

Conversion was a matter for serious consideration with Solanus, not only in the lives of others but especially for his own soul. Sometimes he would say to a visitor, "You pray for my conversion, and I will pray for yours." Again, in a letter: "Only in heaven can we be satisfied as being fully and really converted." Thus he was at all times mindful of his own need to strive after perfection by the practice of virtue.

A novice brother reported how he had seen Solanus running to the office when his call bell rang. The superior, who was standing in the corridor, called out sharply, "Father Solanus! Don't run, slow down." Immediately Solanus stopped, then slowly made his way to the office. Solanus's humble act of obedience made a lasting impression on the novice.

Much evidence of the outstanding virtues in the life of Solanus Casey was recorded in the process of diocesan investigation conducted in Detroit in 1983 and 1984. Several friars spoke of the heroic obedience they had witnessed while living with him. Br. Ignatius Milne stated in his testimony:

> I think Fr. Solanus was imbued with the spirit of obedience. I never found him to criticize or complain or object to the will of

his superior, whether it was fair or unjust. His attitude was that this was the Will of God, and if it was meant to be different, in time it will work out.

I feel he must have really learned this, and certainly gave evidence of the spirit of obedience, when it was determined that he would be ordained but only as a priest-simplex. This must have been a great disappointment to him, and yet he accepted it. It was in this spirit that he accepted every rule, order, command, and commission that was given him. I believe that he promoted the spirit of obedience in others by his great example.[4]

Nine

AN ATTEMPTED RESPITE

*What a horizon for sinners if we but stop and remember
that to know God covers everything.*
—FR. SOLANUS

By the year 1945 the long hours and steady work at the office began to take their toll on Solanus's health. He became more subject to severe colds and even influenza during the winter. A couple of times he had to be hospitalized with pneumonia.

Solanus really needed a rest. An occasion presented itself when he received an invitation to attend the first Mass of one of his nephews, John McCluskey, who was to be ordained a Jesuit priest.

The celebration was scheduled for the end of June 1945 in Seattle, Washington. It was to be a real family reunion for many of the Casey brothers and sisters. The provincial superior readily granted Solanus permission to join his brothers, Fr. Maurice Casey and Msgr. Edward Casey, on the long train trip west.

ANOTHER FAMILY REUNION
Maurice had been recovering from a nervous breakdown at a sanatorium in Baltimore and was ready to return to St. Paul. Solanus had been

quite concerned about him and had decided not to make this trip unless Maurice also was able to go.

Edward had only recently been liberated from a Japanese prison camp in the Philippines and had returned to the United States to recuperate. Now he went to Baltimore with his brothers Owen and Patrick to obtain Maurice's release. They met Solanus in Chicago, and together they all set out for the long journey by train to Seattle.

For the brothers the reunion was a time to relive happy memories. For the rest of the family it was an occasion to get acquainted with their rather famous uncle. Some of the nieces and nephews had never met the "holy Fr. Solanus," of whom they often heard their parents speak. Solanus thoroughly enjoyed the celebrations but often had to endure the reputation of a celebrity. Everybody wanted to see and meet him.

All the attention, however, did not diminish his joy to be with his sisters and brothers. One day there was a boat ride on Lake Washington. Solanus arrived at the dock a little late, so he had to run and then jump, with all the agility of a youth, to catch the boat.

One evening someone brought out a violin, and Solanus played for the family while a nephew recorded his rendition. The recording brings out smiles today, but its charm is in hearing Solanus speak and sing with simple fervor. This recording and another made by friends in Chicago are the only existing records of Fr. Solanus's voice.

Besides the relatives in Seattle, others were anxious to meet Solanus. His brothers arranged a trip to the "City of the Angels," where he was able to meet more of his relatives. One of his nieces, a Sister of the Holy Names of Jesus and Mary, was making a thirty-day retreat. Solanus and Edward stopped in Oregon to see her, but the meeting was brief. Solanus was whisked away to speak to the novices and other sisters at her community's provincial headquarters.

The original two-week vacation time was running out when a difficulty arose in getting return reservations on the train. Solanus wrote to his superior in Detroit and explained the situation. The usual triennial provincial chapter was in session at St. Bonaventure's, and Solanus lamented in his letter the fact that he was missing "the grace of the Chapter."

Fr. Marion Roessler wired back, extending the vacation time by one week. But because of the wartime travel conditions, it took more than that to get back to Detroit. By the time he returned the chapter was over.

Among the personnel changes that had been decided at the chapter meeting was a transfer for Solanus. He was to move away from the crushing burdens of work in Detroit to a quieter place, St. Michael's Monastery in Brooklyn, New York.

RETIREMENT?

Solanus arrived back from the West on a Saturday and found instructions to be in Brooklyn the following Monday. After twenty-one years in Detroit with a host of friends who loved him, he was suddenly leaving. Without a word of complaint or question about the change, he left with only a few items of clothing. He entrusted me to pack up an old trunk with the remaining few clothes, his violin, and some family letters.

At St. Michael's in Brooklyn he immediately took up the duties of porter again. It was a little less work "under the Archangel's wings," as he wrote, but not for long. Soon word went around in New York City that Fr. Solanus Casey was back.

Many New Yorkers remembered the goodness he had spread among them in years past. Now they brought new friends to St. Michael's who would remember Solanus long after he left Brooklyn. When the Father Solanus Guild was organized after his death, these friends in the New York-Brooklyn area became very active members, zealous in promoting his reputation for sainthood.

Before long the doorbell at St. Michael's started ringing almost all day long. More mail was pouring in, and Solanus found that the correspondence was keeping him up late at night. The friars did not seem to realize that he was almost as busy as he had been in Detroit.

Solanus still found time to enjoy his violin. One night he thought he would entertain the brothers. As he proceeded to play a favorite Irish melody, a friar turned on the radio and gradually turned up the volume. Solanus took the hint and moved into the empty church, where he played before the Lord with holy simplicity.

During this time at St. Michael's he suffered something like ulcers. A friend told him that a little garlic every day would be good for his stomach, and Solanus did find it helpful. Before long, however, the superior noticed the unpleasant whiff.

"Don't get any more garlic with the vegetable order," he told the brother cook.

When Solanus noticed they were out of garlic, he mentioned it to the cook. Br. Bonaventure had to tell him that Fr. Superior had said, "No more garlic."

"Well," Solanus replied rather ruefully, "we tried anyway," and he let it go at that.

Meanwhile, the people of Detroit were stunned to lose their benefactor so suddenly. When they found out that Solanus was in Brooklyn, many began phoning to ask his prayers and advice. Some made the long trip to obtain his blessing. Now there was hardly any rest for their good friend. This was not the retirement the superiors had in mind for him.

Hidden Service in Huntington

In less than a year Solanus was sent to a rural community in Huntington, Indiana, this time without any further duties as porter. St. Felix Friary was the novitiate house for the young men entering the order. It seemed an ideal place for retreat from the demands of so many people.

However, word soon reached Detroit that Fr. Solanus was now only two hundred miles away in Indiana. Once again he was at the service of people in need. Phone calls for Solanus, at all hours of the day and night, besieged the monastery.

One night about midnight an old friend in Detroit called to say that his wife was very sick in the hospital. Solanus listened to his plea for prayers and then assured him that his wife would be all right in the morning. Then Solanus exclaimed, "Now tell me, how are the Tigers [Detroit's baseball team] doing?"

Solanus was still a baseball enthusiast. Some days at recreation time the novices would have a game. Solanus liked to watch from the sidelines to cheer. The young friars occasionally invited him to play, and he could still hit a few long flies.

In spite of arthritis and the aches and pains of advancing age, Solanus remained young at heart. He felt right at home in this rural countryside. He relished the memories it brought of his own youth on the farmlands of Wisconsin.

Many families came by car, and soon groups in buses started to descend on the quiet novitiate of St. Felix. To some friars it seemed a disruption of the monastic discipline, but Solanus accepted it all with equanimity.

One superior did take exception to all this attention on the part of visitors. When a bus full of friends from Detroit arrived without prior notice, the superior forbade Solanus to go to the office to meet them. The people were kept waiting in the parking lot almost all day while Solanus remained at prayer in the chapel.

Finally the superior relented a little. He allowed Solanus to bless the people on the bus a few minutes before they had to start their journey back to Detroit. Solanus accepted the humbling incident without a murmur of complaint.

On another occasion a group of pilgrims visiting him had occasion to complain about some action of their local bishop. Solanus could not tolerate such criticism of the church whose representative the bishop was. He roundly scolded the complainers for their lack of love and respect for God's chosen minister.

JUBILEE CELEBRATIONS

During the relatively quiet years at St. Felix, Solanus was able to celebrate two jubilees. In January 1947 he came back to St. Bonaventure Monastery for his golden jubilee as a Capuchin. After a Solemn Mass of thanksgiving in the same little chapel where he first pronounced the vows of poverty, chastity, and obedience, he was given a tumultuous welcome in the Third Order Hall.

The Secular Franciscans had prepared a splendid banquet for all the visitors, who were overjoyed to see him back again. His sister Grace Brady and his brother Owen had come from California, and Msgr. Edward Casey from Minnesota. Many good friends arrived from various distances to express their sincere congratulations and to give thanks for his life and the blessings wrought by his prayers for them.

Seven years later, in July 1954, he celebrated the fiftieth jubilee of his ordination at Huntington. Again a host of friends, together with his brothers Owen and Edward, joined him in a festive liturgy of thanksgiving to God for the grace of a very fruitful priesthood. Two confreres celebrated as deacon and subdeacon at the altar with him, for their silver jubilee as Capuchin priests. When called upon at the banquet to address the happy gathering of well-wishers, Solanus could only voice the constant theme of his whole life, a heartfelt "*Deo gratias*, thanks be to God."

ORA ET LABORA

Day after day in the Huntington years Solanus gave himself to prayer and work. He was often at the office with some troubled person in need of his counsel. Otherwise he might be found in the chapel before the tabernacle, deep in prayer.

At other times he liked to be out in the garden digging weeds or tending the bees that supplied the friars with rich honey. He seemed to be immune to their sting and could go among them without danger. Once when the bees were about to swarm, he soothed them back into the hive with a little concert on his harmonica.

Another time a friar who got too close to the hive was suddenly stung. He was allergic to bee stings and fell down, writhing in pain. Solanus rushed to his side and blessed him. Immediately the friar got up, and he had no further effects of the sting.

Solanus was supposed to be officially retired. Yet he continued his unselfish ministry of prayer and concern for God's people for several more years. His desire was to give his all to God.

Ten

SECRETARIES AND OTHER COLLEAGUES

—What a privilege to do a favor for God in
doing [so] for our neighbor.
FR. SOLANUS

The last years of "retirement" allowed Solanus more time for letter writing, but the amount of correspondence was still more than he could keep up with. Several friars were appointed, one after the other, to serve as his secretary.

The secretary would gather his mail together each day. He would remove any enclosed donations and record them as Mass stipends or Seraphic Mass Association enrollments or whatever the donor stipulated. If a personal reply was not needed, the friar would send a preprinted acknowledgement with the promise of Fr. Solanus's prayers for the person's intentions.

A few letters that seemed more personal were given to Solanus to answer himself. In these later years, typing became very difficult because of arthritis in his fingers, but he would try to type a reply. If he was not interrupted too much, he could produce a long letter with very practical advice. Fr. Blase Gitzen, one of the first secretaries, stated that he was amazed at the profound theological replies that he noticed in the letters he addressed and posted for Solanus.

A Blessed Ministry

Another secretary, Br. Booker Ashe, one of the first African-American friars for the Province of St. Joseph, testified how his work for Solanus brought him blessings and a prophecy:

> I personally went through a great deal of trepidation and indecision within my own self. I think it was through his encouragement that I was able to persevere. He told me that I would make solemn profession, that I would see my twenty-fifth jubilee, and that I would help to bring about a lot of changes in the Province. Now I think that many of those things have really come to pass. He even told me that I would do things that no brother had ever done.[1]

Br. Booker became the first Capuchin brother in modern times to be elected a provincial councilor, serving two terms. He was a respected and influential leader among Black Catholics in America.

Br. Gabriel Badalamenti, another friar who served as secretary to Fr. Solanus, would often tell him about a correspondent's problems or simple requests for prayer. Then Solanus would give a few words of advice that Gabriel could write back to the person. Gabriel testified at the diocesan investigation about Solanus's prudence:

> I believe that Fr. Solanus was a prudent man. I never heard anybody complain about the things they were told to do [by Solanus] or how to do them. He was prudent in giving counsel. After all, most of his counsel was directed towards spiritual things such as attending Mass, receiving the sacraments, prayer, etc.[2]

Br. Gabriel also served as Solanus's nurse when he was ill in Huntington. He brought Solanus to Detroit in 1956, when his health was deteriorating, and attended him at St. John Hospital before his death.

HOLY TRAVEL

During those ten years in Huntington, Solanus came back to Detroit on a few occasions to visit sick friends and benefactors. Usually some friend would drive Solanus by car to Detroit or back again to Huntington. One young man who offered to drive Solanus on a return trip to Huntington was James Maher. He gave an edifying account of that drive when he testified at the diocesan investigation:

> The day that I was to drive him to Huntington, we were delayed because I had to get the brakes fixed on my car. Someone from the monastery drove [Solanus] out to the place where my car was being repaired. The car was ready to go when he arrived, and I thought he would be anxious to leave, but he asked me if there was a church nearby. I told him that Presentation Church was close at hand, so he said, "Let's go over and say some prayers."
>
> We went to the church, and he said, "Let's say the rosary." We said five decades at the church and the other ten decades on the way to Huntington.
>
> In talking to him about my vocation, he told me that I should be faithful to attendance at Mass and if possible to attend Mass during the week and to receive Holy Communion, and, if I could not go to Mass or receive Communion, to make a spiritual communion.
>
> I asked him: "How do you make a spiritual communion?" He said to me, "This is what I say: Lord, please come to me in spiritual communion. Send your Body and Blood gushing through my veins, your love to my heart, my soul, and my mind. Lift me up to your bosom, and infuse me with your Divine Love."
>
> I had one occasion to observe Fr. Solanus eating on our way....We had picked up a hitchhiker and stopped to eat. The man apparently had not eaten in a day or two and was very hungry. Fr. Solanus had fish to eat, and there were three pieces of fish on his plate. I noticed that he pushed one piece to the back of his plate.

He ate very slowly and finished the two small pieces of fish. Then he asked the hitchhiker if he was still hungry. The man said he was, whereupon Fr. Solanus passed him the third piece of fish. It seems to me that from the very beginning he had decided to save that piece for this person.[3]

One of Solanus's favorite practices while on a drive was to say a rosary with the driver and passengers. Once he was a little late joining a group of friars leaving St. Felix. Because he caused a delay, the superior punished Solanus by declaring that now they would not have a rosary on the way. He was saddened by this lack of devotion but said not a word of complaint or criticism.

FURTHER LESSONS IN HUMILITY

Solanus always accepted with good grace these little barbs or humiliations given by a few friars. He followed the advice he once offered to a person in a letter: "If we want to acquire the virtue of humility, we must undergo humiliations."

The humbling misadventures of his own brother, Fr. Maurice Casey, became a lesson in humility for Solanus. For many years Maurice had been unhappy in his parish assignments, but he finally found contentment at Holy Trinity Hospital in Graceville, Minnesota, where he served as part-time chaplain and eventually became a patient. Solanus felt relieved and grateful for Maurice's serenity at last. When Solanus received news of Maurice's peaceful death on January 12, 1949, he accepted it as divinely providential.

With permission to attend the funeral, Solanus started out alone on the long train trip and arrived at Holy Rosary Parish rectory before dawn. Not wishing to wake the pastor so early, he decided to wait on the cold porch. Fortunately the pastor heard him and brought him in for a warm breakfast.

Msgr. Edward Casey celebrated the Solemn Requiem Mass, which was attended by Bishop Byrne of St. Paul and fifteen diocesan priests. Solanus preached on the text "What shall I render to the Lord for all the things He hath rendered to me?" (Ps 115). In the words of Edward, "His sermon was a meditation on death for the faithful Christian; the humiliating, purifying gateway to eternal life; the last of the blessings that God showers on our earthly journey to heaven." It was the only time that Solanus was able to attend the funeral of a family member.

In April 1949 Solanus made a journey of particular significance but with some rather unfortunate results for him. He accompanied a group of friars from St. Felix to Milwaukee for the dedication of a large granite statue of his friend and coworker Fr. Stephen Eckert.

Fr. Stephen had a reputation for sanctity. He established the St. Benedict Mission for African-American people in Milwaukee. He died in 1923, and his remains were entombed at the mission in 1948. At the luncheon following the ceremonies, the ham that was served had spoiled. A number of the laypeople and friars, including Solanus, suffered ptomaine poisoning. Solanus had to spend several days in the hospital before he could return to Huntington.

Solanus's good friends continued to shower him with esteem and often with gifts that were of great benefit to the St. Felix Community. Once, when the friary was in need of a car, the superior asked Solanus's help. Solanus approached a friend—a car dealer in Detroit—and the friars promptly received a new Chevrolet. Another friend who had obtained help through Fr. Solanus's prayers donated a large laundry machine for the monastery, out of gratitude to God.

In spite of all the gifts of grateful friends, Solanus made little use of material things. He looked upon everything as given for the good of the community. True to his vow of poverty, he was content with the barest necessities, patched and worn clothing and the simple fare of the monastery table.

Confronting Atheism

During the 1950s there was much news about unsettling world events, especially the rise of communism and its avowed atheism. Solanus was attuned to the times and very much aware of world events. He expressed his thoughts in a letter to a fellow religious:

> God bless you and yours these days—at once—days of threatening forebodings, and God's outstanding mercies. God bless our poor modern humanity, with all its wonderful gifts; but alas! with its innumerable weaknesses and its appalling absurdities, atheism, the chief, unholy parent of them all.[4]

He felt that the greatest danger of the time was the atheism of communism. He just could not imagine how anyone could not believe in God. He wanted people to understand the folly of atheism and expressed this view freely, as in the following excerpt from an essay:

> To every normal thinking mind, atheism, by its very nature, has always been considered nothing less than a blasphemous suggestion of the devil. This, however, does not exactly cap the monster. For whereas man's purpose as a rational creature is to recognize and to know the creator, so as to be able intelligently to love Him, confidently to hope in Him, and gratefully to serve Him, this monster, atheism, by trying to weaken belief in God and the supernatural and rob us entirely of holy faith in Almighty God, would poison everything pertaining to these virtues so essential to our happiness. Atheism is the climax of intellectual and moral insanity—the hopeless conclusion and desperate refuge at once of shallow thinking, of degenerate minds and fools.[5]

To another friend he wrote the following strong condemnation:

> God bless you and yours these days of grace. Days of God's great mercy to all people of good will, notwithstanding our lamentable want of appreciation and gratitude for God's uncountable favors. Days of grace too, notwithstanding the threatening avalanche of international red-atheism even now bedeviling millions of humanity more and more.
>
> Atheism! God help us. The social octopus, cancer of mind and spirit,...atheism, the stifler of every phase of science...that has fostered gratitude to parents and benefactors as to God's representatives, and that instead of hope, the very soul of happiness in this world, would inject the poisonous nightmare of despair.[6]

Solanus became so concerned about the evil effects of atheism that he tried to initiate an essay contest to make people more aware of its danger for souls:

> A million-dollar essay-proposition: [Conducted] in order to rescue from despair the hopes and souls of billions. Hope, the very soul of happiness in this world—despair, a first foretaste of hell. "Know the truth, and the truth shall make you free."
>
> [A contest] for the best popular definition and contrasting of the two extremes of most fundamental importance—religion, the unrecognized science—and atheism, the climax of intellectual insanity and of moral depravity. Said definitions not to exceed fifteen hundred words and to avoid undue reference to any particular system or denomination.[7]

It was a bold proposition. It revealed how imbued he was with supernatural faith and how he wanted all people to come to the saving knowledge of God. He posed the idea to his superiors and to several friends who he thought would be glad to donate the prize. But he was unable to stir their interest and so had to abandon the idea. It was a valiant effort, an indication of his undying missionary zeal.

Eleven

The Sacrifice of Self

*How short the joys of earth—and the sorrows too! Thank
God, what a glorious contrast in heaven.*
—Fr. Solanus

Solanus's last years at Huntington were plagued with health problems.
The skin condition that had affected his legs for many years became so
bad that he had to be hospitalized several times.

The doctors at the hospital in Fort Wayne, Indiana, not far from
Huntington, were unable to find a cure or any way to relieve the pain.
Once the doctors even considered amputation, but the condition
improved a little. Solanus was able to return to the friary, but not for long.

In January of 1956 the condition flared up again. The provincial superior, Gerald Walker, decided to send Solanus back to Detroit, where more
advanced medical help was available. This was to be his final transfer, the
beginning of a long journey to greater holiness through the crucible of
suffering.

Until now Solanus had spent his life helping others through their trials
and pains. Now God was calling him to the ultimate sacrifice of everything until—according to his heart's desire—there would be nothing left
to give.

When Fr. Gerald transferred him back to St. Bonaventure Monastery, it was with the hope that his health might improve. This time he was to have complete rest and no contact with the people. It was a difficult decision, and hard for Solanus as well.

Although the friars tried to keep his presence hidden, it soon became known. Solanus could easily forget his own needs; he wanted to be available for others. Yet he would not go against the superior's orders.

Special Visits

From time to time exceptions were made. Br. Richard Merling, director of the Father Solanus Guild for more than twenty-five years, has given an account of a very special visit he had with Solanus the Sunday before Christmas in 1956.

Richard's brother Ray had injured his leg in an auto accident, and it was not healing. His mother, a nurse, had known Fr. Solanus for many years. Her father, Ed Traynor, was a brother of Tom Traynor, who had married Solanus's sister Ellen.

Mrs. Merling called Br. Gerard Geromette, porter at the monastery, who had been her patient at Holy Cross Hospital. Gerard prevailed upon the superior to allow the Merling family to visit Solanus. Richard, then in his teens, together with his mother and father and sister Lois, waited in a small office room. Soon Solanus came in. He was happy to see them.

Mrs. Merling proceeded to tell Solanus about Ray's injury and the lack of healing. Solanus assured them that Ray's leg would heal and that they should not worry. He seemed glad of the visit and spoke a little about his family and their life on the farm.

Then Solanus said that he had just restrung his violin and offered to play for them. As Br. Richard recalled, they didn't notice Solanus's faulty playing but enjoyed it.

Before Solanus was ready to leave them, he wanted to bless them all. When he came to Richard he seemed to make a special blessing. Richard feels today that Solanus's blessing may have fostered his vocation to the Capuchins seven years later.

Other people approached the porters, Br. Ignatius Milne and Br. Gabriel Badalamenti, asking for a chance to see Solanus. In spite of his precarious health, permission was occasionally granted. Solanus was only too glad to be of service to the sick. He readily listened to their stories of trouble and seemed to lose all sense of time as he tried to encourage their faith and trust in God. All his strength was still at the service of the Lord.

THE PATIENT PATIENT

Solanus was placed under the care of Dr. John A. Maloney at first. Eventually Dr. Maloney asked Dr. William B. McIntyre, on the staff of St. John Hospital, to take over Solanus's care because St. John was nearer the monastery. This could be an important factor in the event of an emergency.

The skin affliction that had troubled Solanus's legs for many years now began to spread over his entire body. It was diagnosed as severe erysipelas. Because Solanus was allergic to the known antibiotics of the time, there was very little the doctors could do to help him.

In May of 1956 he was hospitalized for about a week, improved a little, and was sent home. For the next year he was in and out of the hospital. Other patients would hear of his stays and would sneak into his room for a blessing. To their great joy, they often experienced his healing intercession for them.

The Sisters of St. Joseph, in charge of the hospital, also revered their famous patient and enjoyed his sense of humor. One day a sister came into his room and asked, "How about a blessing?"

"All right," he said playfully, "I'll take one."

Sometimes he invited the sisters to pray the rosary with him or read to him from his favorite work, *The Mystical City of God.*

When his condition improved even a little, he would return to the monastery and try to follow the monastic schedule. He took no thought of his weak condition but applied himself to prayer and a little work outdoors. He even tried to get in a little exercise, walking briskly in the monastery yard.

In January 1957, his health much better, the community held a little celebration to honor the sixtieth anniversary of his profession as a Capuchin. Kneeling at the same altar where he had made his commitment to God the first time, he renewed his vows of poverty, chastity, and obedience. He was so overcome with tears of joy that a confrere had to finish the formula of profession for him. The gift of his whole life as a Capuchin and a priest was the constant source of a holy joy and of his spirit of gratitude.

Two months later Solanus recalled the pleasant memory in a letter to his brother Edward:

> Thanks be to God, though comparatively unnoted and quiet, God granted us the gracious privilege to celebrate a happy diamond jubilee in the order and in the holy habit of St. Francis.
>
> This took place Monday, January 14, at solemn high Mass. I would hardly know how it could have been more beautiful. I had come to the holy novitiate Christmas Eve [1896]. It was six months ahead of the seven other students, who joined me the following July. They are all gone to heaven now, we hope, with the senior of them all, Fr. Damasus, in his ninetieth year. Had he waited [for death] five months longer, he and I would have had our golden jubilee together. He was patient and joyful to the last. May he be privileged to await, in the peace of the saints, the inconceivable glory of the general resurrection.[1]

LOOKING AHEAD WITH HOPE

Solanus's digression on death in his letter to Edward reveals his own solid hope in the resurrection. In many of his letters he speaks of the beauty of death and how we should look forward to it. For example: "Many are the rainbows, the sunbursts, the gentle breezes—and the hailstorms we are liable to meet before, by the grace of God, we shall be able to tumble into our graves with the confidence of tired children into their places of peaceful slumber."

Another letter has this: "Let us prepare for our final moment on earth by patient suffering, prayer, and the sacraments, then we will receive with joyful countenance the final call of the Divine Lover—the Bridegroom of our souls—and gently pass into eternity."

Throughout his life he had fostered a healthy, hope-filled view of death. As a young priest in Yonkers he once declared to his friend Willie Spring, "Death can be beautiful—like a wedding—if we make it so."

A letter written in 1946 to his niece Helena Wilhite reveals his confidence in God's loving providence: "Let us thank God ahead of time for whatever He foresees is pleasing to Him,... leaving everything at His divine disposal, including—with all its circumstances, when, where, and how—God may be pleased to dispose the events of our death."

In his last days his prayers were, as usual, for the needs of the sick and troubled but not for the relief of his own sufferings. Now he longed only for a happy death.

He found joy in attending extra Masses and even in serving another priest's Mass. Fr. Michael Dalton from Canada told of his happy meeting with Solanus in 1957, while saying Mass at St. Bonaventure's:

> I said Mass in the monastery chapel, and a very elderly friar served my Mass. I did not know then that he was a priest. I was quite impressed when I saw him kneel and kiss the floor when he passed in front of the tabernacle. I thought it very devout and humble.

After Mass he took me in for breakfast. Taking me down a long monastery hall, he went into a room with the name "Fr. Solanus" over the door. When I saw who he was, I asked him to hear my confession. He is the only priest in seventy-five years who refused [me] absolution, saying, "I'm only a simplex priest—no faculties to absolve."

He told me, however, that his work in the office, meeting troubled humanity, was similar to confession. He talked at breakfast of being a streetcar operator in his youth. At eighty-six years he was my oldest altar boy.[2]

THE FINAL GIFT

At St. Bonaventure's Solanus was able to spend time in quiet contemplation without the interruptions of former times. In April of 1957 I had the good fortune to be stationed again in Detroit after spending five years in Wisconsin. I was happy to be with Solanus again, happy to serve him at Mass and in other ways. I was able to give him a little comfort by reading from *The Mystical City of God* when his eyes pained him.

As this last year progressed, his strength and stamina diminished. On the Feast of the Sacred Heart, June 28, 1957, he said Mass privately in a small oratory next to the monastery chapel. Br. Casper Rodich served for the Mass and noticed what a struggle it was for Solanus. It was to be the last time he would offer the Holy Sacrifice.

He became so weak that four days later he had to be taken to St. John Hospital again. The erysipelas now covered his entire body. The only remedy for the burning pain was to gently bathe him with oil, but even that gave very little relief. The friars visited him as often as they could. They marveled at his patient suffering. He never complained.

A couple of days before Solanus died, he told Fr. Gerald, "I look on my whole life as giving, and I want to give and give until there is nothing left of me to give."

Another time he said to Fr. Gerald, "I am offering my suffering that we might all be one. Oh, if I could only live to see the conversion of the whole world."

When Br. Ignatius noticed his sufferings, he said, "Oh, Father, you must be in great pain."

Though very weak Solanus responded, "Would to God it were ten thousand times worse so that I would have something to offer God in thanksgiving."

During his last few days friars, sisters, nurses, and friends were often at Solanus's side. On July 29 Mrs. Martha Casey, wife of his deceased brother Owen, came from California to offer assistance as a nurse. When he saw her, Solanus exclaimed, "Oh, Martha, I knew you would come, and on your feast day, too!"

On the morning of July 31 Msgr. Edward Casey, who had been spending a few days with Solanus, thought he seemed to rally a little. He left the room to write a report to the family. About that time a nurse and an orderly came in to bathe Solanus with oil. When they finished, they gently laid him back on the pillow. They heard him softly whisper something, but they could not understand him.

Suddenly he sat up, stretched out his arms, and in a clear voice said, "I give my soul to Jesus Christ." These were his last words.

Lying back on the pillow, he breathed forth his soul. It was eleven o'clock in the morning, at the very hour and on the very date of his first Holy Mass, fifty-three years before. The sisters and the doctors, with Msgr. Edward, were consoled on entering the room to see the look of peace on Solanus's face.

THE CITY MOURNS

Within moments the word went around the hospital, "Father Solanus just died." The friars were notified before any announcement was made to the city, but it seemed that already all Detroit knew of and mourned the passing of their holy friend.

The funeral director, Arthur Van Lerberghe, personal friend of Solanus and the friars, immediately made arrangements for his burial. Those preparing the body were amazed to find that all traces of the skin disease that had covered his body had disappeared.

Solanus died on a Wednesday, so it was decided to have him laid in state at the funeral parlor on Thursday afternoon. At seven o'clock in the morning people already were lined up waiting to enter the funeral home to pay their last respects to one who was everybody's friend. The long lines of people continued all day Thursday and again all day Friday, when the body lay in state before the sanctuary in St. Bonaventure Church.

Msgr. Edward Casey celebrated the funeral Mass on Saturday morning, August 2, 1957, at ten o'clock, with Bishop Henry E. Donnelly and many priests in attendance. Mount Elliott Street in front of the monastery was closed to traffic, and the sidewalks were jammed with people who could not find room in the church.

Fr. Gerald Walker preached the homily. With great emotion he said, "His was a life of service and love for people like you and me....He had a divine love for people. He loved people for what he could do for them— and for God, through them." His glowing words were echoed many times in the various tributes that appeared in the daily newspapers.

After the final prayers the long procession of mourners filed past the monastery to the friars' own cemetery within the monastery garden. There the body of Fr. Solanus Casey was laid to rest. A simple stone bearing his name and years marked his grave, in no way different from those of the other friars resting there.

Over the years his grave has become a place of pilgrimage, visited by hundreds of people. Visitors continue to find comfort and healing through the intercession of one they consider "their saint." People come in all kinds of weather and from varying distances to pray at this holy place.

Numerous reports are on file today about wonderful favors received by people who have visited the simple grave of Solanus Casey. His reputation for holiness continues to spread to all parts of America and to other countries of the world, bringing hope and faith to many.

Epilogue

THE CAUSE FOR CANONIZATION

When the news of Solanus Casey's death on July 31, 1957, became known, the Detroit City Council passed a testimonial resolution, which read in part:

> Whereas, the City of Detroit with profound sorrow expresses regret in the passing of Rev. Fr. Solanus Casey, advisor to thousands of troubled persons,...who won his many followers mainly as a spiritual guide,...be it resolved that the members of the Common Council of the City of Detroit take this opportunity to express their deep regret in the passing of so loved a person.[1]

The Detroit newspapers—as they had done frequently during his lifetime—carried many articles in praise of Fr. Solanus and his good work. Headlines included "Fr. Solanus, Advisor to Thousands, Dies" and "Famed Priest Helped Feed Souls and Stomachs in the Depression."

The Michigan Catholic, a diocesan paper, said in part:

> Sixty years a Capuchin friar, fifty-three years a priest, a potent, persuasive counselor and comforter to thousands beset by physical, mental, and spiritual tribulations, Fr. Solanus Casey, died Wednesday morning in St. John's Hospital here. Fr. Solanus was active for twenty-one years at St. Bonaventure's Monastery. In that time he became widely known as the friend and helper of people

in need, whether spiritual or material. He gave sound advice and spiritual consolation to many. He helped the sick and procured aid or work for others. No one went away unaided.[2]

PROCLAIMING THE TRUTH

Early in 1958 Fr. Gerald Walker sent to the minister general in Rome the necrology of Fr. Solanus, at the end of which he wrote:

> As we attended his funeral, we could not help but think that there lies a man who lived almost eighty-seven years of life without tasting the good things of the world. It was not because he hated the good things God has made. It was not because he could not appreciate their beauty and desirability, but it was because he so loved Christ and souls that he could not allow anything else to come in between. Recognizing his utter poverty, his privation of everything, with scarcely enough flesh to cover his bones, one who does not love God would say: "Silly monk, crazy Capuchin." But it is my firm conviction that God will yet proclaim the truth about Fr. Solanus to the world.[3]

In response to Fr. Walker's report, the minister general, Fr. Benignus of Sant' Ilario, wrote of his great admiration for Solanus:

> Fr. Solanus was certainly an extraordinary man, a replica of St. Francis, a real Capuchin. The wonderful spontaneous tribute paid to him by Catholic and non-Catholic alike is surely an ample proof that our traditional spirituality is still very much capable of winning the people among whom we work to a realization of the primacy of the spiritual and Catholic outlook on life. May he still continue to do much good from heaven, bringing many souls nearer to God and inspiring his own Capuchin brothers with something of his humble spirit.[4]

By 1960 many reports concerning the outstanding virtues of Fr. Solanus Casey were coming to the friars at St. Bonaventure's Monastery in Detroit. There were so many people who had experienced Fr. Solanus's help, either while he lived or after his death, that they wanted some way to preserve his memory. On May 8, 1960, a group of these devoted friends met to discuss organizing a guild in his memory.

On July 31, 1960, the third anniversary of his holy death, the Father Solanus Guild had its first membership meeting, with the approval of the minister provincial. Its stated purpose is to keep alive the inspiring memory of Fr. Solanus Casey and to collect and disseminate information about his life, especially his work on behalf of the poor and the missions.

When a Detroit author heard about Solanus's wonderful works, he felt that here was a life story that needed to be written. James Derum spent seven years researching and interviewing many people who had known Fr. Solanus, including some relatives. He spent a week in Wisconsin with Msgr. Edward Casey, who gave many details about the early life of Solanus.

Derum's painstaking work became the first biography of Solanus Casey. Published by the Father Solanus Guild in 1968, it is titled *The Porter of St. Bonaventure's*.

Considering Canonization

Within a short time a movement was started to consider Solanus as a candidate for canonization. The Detroit Capuchins were reluctant at first to consider canonization for one of their own. But finally, at the urging of the Guild members, the next provincial minister, Fr. Gerard Hesse, sent a report of Fr. Solanus's reputation for sanctity to the general minister in Rome. His report included an account of twenty-four cases of healing attributed to the intercession of Solanus Casey.

This detailed report of Solanus's holiness of life and of the many favors attributed to his prayers moved the general superiors to open the cause for canonization. On October 4, 1966, the Capuchin postulator for causes of saintly Capuchins, Fr. Berardine Romagnoli, appointed as vice-postulator Fr. Paschal Siler, a Capuchin stationed at St. Bonaventure Monastery in Detroit.

A vice-postulator serves as the delegate of the postulator in Rome to collect on the local level all the information about the life and virtue of a person being considered for sainthood. The vice-postulator must also work with the bishop or archbishop of the place where the saintly person died and was buried, because it is the local bishop who has jurisdiction over an official investigation concerning the holiness of a Servant of God. The bishop acts on behalf of the Congregation for the Causes of the Saints at the Vatican.

Fr. Paschal began by contacting people who had stories about how Fr. Solanus had helped them physically or spiritually in times of trouble. Several members of the Father. Solanus Guild assisted the vice-postulator in collecting reports concerning Solanus's life of virtue and his powerful intercession on behalf of suffering people.

In 1973 the provincial chapter transferred Fr. Paschal to the Native American Missions in Montana, thus ending his work on the cause. In July 1974 I was appointed to succeed Fr. Paschal as vice-postulator. I continued to prepare the documentation needed for the introduction of the cause of canonization for Solanus Casey.

THE CAUSE TAKES SHAPE

One of the important steps in the process of a cause for sainthood is to collect any known writings of a Servant of God. By a decree of January 1977, Cardinal John Dearden, archbishop of Detroit, requested that all writings of Fr. Solanus Casey be sent to the chancery offices of the Detroit archdiocese. Two theological censors in the Detroit archdiocese carefully examined the body of writings and declared them free of any doctrinal error. When these writings were assembled and transcribed, they were bound into four volumes and turned over to the Postulator General in Rome.

Official approval to open the cause was granted on June 19, 1982. On September 21, 1983, the new archbishop of Detroit, Edmund C. Szoka, issued the decree, opening the diocesan investigation into the life and virtues of the Servant of God Solanus Casey.

From October 1983 to September 1984, fifty-three witnesses who had known Fr. Solanus personally over time were called to testify, giving examples of his extraordinary virtue. These witnesses—priests, religious, and laypeople—had vivid recollections of Fr. Solanus's kindly concern for people's spiritual and material needs and problems. They were able to offer concrete examples of Solanus's practice of extraordinary virtue. On October 13, 1984, with the investigation completed, over thirty-six thousand typed pages of testimony were presented to the Congregation for the Causes of the Saints.

Another important step was the exhumation and canonical examination of Fr. Solanus's body. Exhumation is necessary to positively identify the remains of a Servant of God. On July 8, 1987, the grave of Fr. Solanus was opened, and the casket was brought into the friars' chapel.

After thirty years of burial the body of Solanus was found to be almost 95 percent intact. The body had been embalmed, but the three doctors who officially examined it felt that the state of preservation was indeed remarkable.

Clothed in a new habit, the body was placed in a new metal casket and interred in a cement crypt beneath the floor in the north transept of St. Bonaventure's Church. Pilgrims came, and continue to come almost daily, from around the country to pray at the tomb for Solanus's intercession.

The cause moved another step forward with the appointment by the Congregation of a Relator for the Cause, Fr. Peter Gumpel, SJ. He in turn appointed Fr. Michael Crosby, OFM Cap, to be his collaborator in preparing the *positio* for the Cause.

This *positio*, or "position paper," covered in great detail Solanus's life, work, and times. It included all the testimonies together with an in-depth analysis of his virtues. The completed work, in three volumes, was given to the Congregation for the Causes of Saints in 1992. Their study was completed in June of 1995, with an affirmative decision.

VENERABLE SOLANUS CASEY

The cardinals and bishops of the Congregation met with Pope John Paul II on July 11, 1995, for the promulgation of the Decree of Heroic Virtue, bestowing on Fr. Solanus Casey the title of Venerable. The declaration of the practice of heroic virtue is the most important step for sainthood. However, public devotion is not allowed until the solemn beatification by the Holy Father. This requires evidence of at least one miracle, verified by a panel of medical experts and theologians.

When Solanus's cause was recommended to the Congregation, the Relator stated, in part,

> While Fr. Solanus's example is relevant for all priests and religious, it would seem to be such in a particular manner for all Americans. They will be able to derive from his life an inspiration entirely based on faith and charity, and at the same time, also deeply human: sociable, optimistic and cheerful, compassionate and active in trying to alleviate the spiritual and material sufferings of others.[5]

During the diocesan investigation Fr. Blase Gitzen had been asked the final question, "Do you have anything more to add?" Blase had stated:

> If Fr. Solanus becomes a saint, we could relate to him very, very well. He is the sort of saint we need today. He never had any great understanding of theological controversy; he just had an understanding

of the goodness of God, the love of God, the graciousness of God, the willingness to help on the part of God.

And he tried to explain that to people; he tried to get it across to them. In most cases he succeeded beautifully. If people came away from him at all, it was with a greater knowledge of a good God. And that was everybody. He accepted sinner, he accepted saint alike....

I am positive that what he did, he attracted more sinners back to God with his kindness and his love and his own gentleness, with his own graciousness toward every human being, than all the preachers did with their bombastic hell and damnation.

He was such a gentle man. Anybody who remembers him remembers how kind he was. They may not remember his words; they may not even have fully understood everything he said to them when he talked to them, but they came away with the impression that this was truly a man of God who loved them. And if he could love them so much, then the Father, God, could love them even more.[6]

We might say that Fr. Blase's response expresses the sentiments of all who have ever met Fr. Solanus Casey.

BLESSED SOLANUS CASEY

The Church requires an officially recognized miracle before beatification can take place. In the case of Solanus Casey, a woman suffering from an incurable genetic skin disease was healed after praying at his tomb and asking for his intercession. The Vatican takes its investigation of miracles seriously, interviewing doctors and scientists to ensure the cure has no scientific explanation.

On May 4, 2017 Pope Francis announced that Father Solanus passed the rigorous test assigned to the process of sainthood, being elevated from Venerable to Blessed by the Roman Catholic Church.

"The beatification of Father Solanus Casey is an incomparable grace for the Church in the Archdiocese of Detroit and for the whole community of Southeast Michigan," stated Archbishop Allen H. Vigneron, Archdiocese of Detroit. "He is an inspiration to all us Catholics—and to all—of the power of grace to transform one's life."

On November 18, 2017 in Detroit's Ford Field, the Mass of Beatification was celebrated in the presence of more than 60,000 people.

For Fr. Solanus to be declared a saint, a second miracle after the beatification was announced would need to be documented and approved by Rome.

NOVENA TO BLESSED SOLANUS CASEY

Leader: Loving Creator God, you are holy, the source of all holiness.

All: We give you thanks for all the ways your holiness shines forth in the humble life of our Capuchin Brother, Blessed Solanus Casey. Help us to not simply admire him but to learn from him—so we too may become like him, open to all the graces God is giving to us on our earthly pilgrimage. We pray in his own spirit, echoing his own words and experience.

Leader: We praise you, O God, for creating us, bringing us into our families and this beautiful but very fragile planet earth.

All: "Blessed be God in all his designs."

Leader: We praise you, O God, for sending us your own Son Jesus, to give himself completely to us as our Savior and our Brother.

All: "Jesus Christ, the Lover of our souls!"

Leader: We praise you, O God, for gifting us with faith, for living in us and making us part of the Church, the Body of Christ on earth.

All: "How little we appreciate our incalculable privileges—the blessings of our holy faith."

Leader: We praise you, O God, for sending your Spirit to guide us every step of the way on our journey of life.

All: "God is so good—oh, thank God a million times!"

Leader: We praise you, O God, for giving us your own Mother to be our Mother and Protector.

All: "Learn to know Mary that you may love heaven and heavenly things."

Leader: We praise you, O God, for giving us experiences throughout our lives to let us know your presence and your call.

All: "How can we ever thank God enough for his merciful guidance?"

Leader: We praise you, O God, for constantly forgiving us when we pay no attention to your guidance and choose sinful paths instead.

All: "God's merciful love is above all his works."

Leader: We praise you, O God, for the gift of vocation: single life, marriage, religious life and priesthood.

All: "How sublime are our vocations!"

Leader: We praise you, O God, for the gift of the Eucharist, drawing us again and again into your own Sacrificial loving.

All: You give us "Your Body and Blood gushing through our veins."

Leader: We praise you, O God, for the gift of our neighbors, especially those who, like Solanus' parents, are Immigrants or refugees, all who are poor and sick and struggling to make ends meet.

All: "What a privilege it is to help one another!"

Leader: We praise you, O God, for the gift of sharing your cross with us through setbacks and hardships.

All: "Be faithful to God in the present moment or you will frustrate the designs of God."

Leader: We praise you, O God, for the loving plan you have for each of us in our living and our dying.

All: "I give my soul to Jesus Christ!"

Leader: We praise you, O God, for your desire to have each of us with you and Blessed Solanus forever in heaven.

All: "We thank God ahead of time!"

Leader: Dear Lord, you are so good, so loving to us all.

All: Our Capuchin Brother Blessed Solanus was filled with gratitude and appreciation for all your gifts and invites us to do the same. Help us to imitate his faith-filled example so that we and our weary world will know the blessings of greater peace, greater hope and joy. This we ask through Christ, our Lord. Amen.

Prayer written by Fr. Dan Crosby, OFM Cap.

Canonization Prayer

O God, I adore You. I give myself to You.
May I be the person You want me to be,
and May Your will be done in my life today.

I thank You for the gifts You gave Father Solanus.
If it is Your Will, bless us with the canonization of
Father Solanus so that others may imitate
and carry on his love for all the poor and
suffering of our world.

As he joyfully accepted Your divine plans,
I ask You, according to Your Will,
to hear my prayer for... *(your intention)*
through Jesus Christ our Lord. Amen.

"Blessed be God in all His Designs."

Imprimatur:
The Most Reverend Allen H. Vigneron
Archbishop of Detroit
May 2017

Wisdom from Fr. Solanus

These inspiring quotations taken from the *Collected Writings of Father Solanus Casey* were selected and arranged by Br. Ignatius Milne in 1978. The original unpublished works are found in the Vice-Postulation Archives in Detroit, Michigan.

Holiness of Life

Man's purpose as a rational creature is to recognize and to know His Creator, so as to be able intelligently to love Him, confidently to hope in Him, and gratefully to serve Him.

Inasmuch as individuals or humanity as a whole turn away from God to seek peace elsewhere, in just so much will they be restless, disappointed, and discouraged.

We must be faithful to the present moment, or we will frustrate the plan of God for our lives.

The weaknesses we experience are naturally providential guards against one of the very greatest dangers to holiness: pride.

Charity is the fountain of supernatural confidence, of hope, of happiness.

Disregard for the claims of justice, under whatever pretext, has always been a manifestation of (to say the very least) shallow thinking—or rather a betrayal of real thinking.

Like the Holy Trinity, faith, hope, and charity are one. Theoretically, faith—like the Eternal Father—comes first; but in both cases, they are essentially one.

Be as blind as possible to the faults of your neighbors, trying at least to attribute a good intention to their actions.

Let us pray for one another's conversion, for no one is fully converted here on this side of heaven.

God often permits us to make temporal blunders in order to foster humility in our souls, so that in the sight of heaven we may be more amiable.

Happiness in this world consists in the hopes we foster. Little children are happy in the vivid hopes that animate them. Ours should be the hope of the saints, springing from the infallible promises of heaven, and imbued with the appreciation of the contrast between the eternal and the temporal.

To practice no religion is making a secondary matter of the primary purpose of our creation as rational beings: to know God, so that we may serve Him and be happy with Him in heaven.

In His divine economy, God has honored His creatures—most especially His rational ones—by giving them each, according to his ability, a part of His own work to do, by participation in His own divine activity.

God is constantly planning wonders for the patient and the humble.

Life here in the exile is so short and uncertain, that it seems to me it ought to have another name.

What a marvelously different society we'd have here, and what an ideal world to live in, if we'd all keep in mind the assurance of Jesus: "What you have done to the least of My brethren, you have done to Me."

It is really a privilege to help one another and to save our neighbors a step, whoever they may be. Since we have nothing of our own, what we do is sure to come back to us again.

Redemption and hope in the final purpose of our existence: to know Him, our blessed Beginning, our Life, and our All.

God's mercy is above all his works, and His patience is essentially one with His mercy.

Let us not worry about past stupidities and sins, but rather thank God for having rescued us from hell and from the jaws of our unruly passions.

This poor sinner Solanus, who more than anyone else gives me the most trouble. I consider it a mercy that we need examine one conscience only!

Blessed be God in all His designs! It is to this little Christian greeting that I am trying to attune my soul, and to echo and resound it to all humanity.

Jesus is no crank! He knows we are not angels but poor sinners, and He understands when we fail.

Everyone who believes in Christ and tries to follow Him is a missionary.

We should ever be grateful for and love the vocation to which God has called us. This applies to every vocation because, after all, what a privilege it is to serve God, even in the least capacity!

FAITH AND CONFIDENCE IN GOD
If we look at things in the light of faith, the worst—as the world considers things—will turn out [to be] our victory.

We are so weak in faith—setting limits to God's power and goodness. Confidence is the very soul of prayer.

We worry our heads and hearts about many things, and almost totally undervalue the invitation most beautiful of all: "Learn of Me, because I am meek and humble of heart." Mary the penitent understood it well, and Jesus praised her for her appreciation.

Humanity's sad weakness: lack of faith and, consequently, want of confidence in God.

Confidence in God—the very soul of courage—is victory assured.

We worry and fret about tomorrow as though our dear Lord had never spoken a word about His divine providence, or proved His loving solicitude for each of us a thousand times a day.

Keep courage—rather, confidence in God, which is courage divinely reinforced.

Shake off excessive worry and show a little confidence in God's merciful providence.

How wonderful the ways of the good God when we foster confidence in Him by leaving something that seems important for Him to take care of.

Worry is a weakness from which very few of us are entirely free. We must be on guard against this most insidious enemy of our peace of soul. Instead let us foster confidence in God, and thank Him ahead of time for whatever He chooses to send us.

God loves to load confidently loving souls with supernatural divine generosity.

The thing the world calls "life" is so short after all, and the hereafter so eternal, that nothing here ought to really disturb us.

Unpleasant situations will always come out right if we only have a little confidence in the good God and our Blessed Mother.

Shake off anxiety. Last year it was something that you smile about now. Tomorrow it's about something that will not be serious if you raise your heart to God and thank Him for whatever comes.

CHURCH AND SACRAMENTS

God could have founded the Church and left it under the supervision of angels that have no human faults and weaknesses. But who can doubt that as it stands today, consisting of and under poor sinners— successors of ignorant fishermen—the Church is a more outstanding miracle than in any other way?

The sacrament of baptism divinely infuses into the soul the triune virtues of faith, hope, and charity, making it a candidate for the life of eternal glory.

When we were baptized, we became candidates for heaven, and every time we receive the sacraments of Mother Church, we take another step forward. How wonderful and legion are our privileged opportunities!

Frequent Communion brings peace into a family and into the soul. It also fosters faith in God and heavenly relationships with all God's dear ones in heaven.

How often I regret that daily Holy Communion was not recommended when we were young! I feel now that we missed so much that would have strengthened us against the dangers and temptations of youth.

As manifested in the lives of the saints, if we strive and use the means God has given us, we too can ascend to great sanctity and to an astonishing familiarity with God—even here—as pilgrims [on our way] to the Beatific Vision.

CROSSES AND SUFFERINGS

Music of the cross—how beautiful when mastered!

Crosses—the best school wherein to learn appreciation for the love of Jesus crucified, the divine Lover of our souls.

We want to be Christians—spouses of Jesus—risen and glorified, of course, but without getting too near the Cross.

We do well to remember how very short, after all, it is till our suffering and our time of merit, too, will be over. Let us offer everything, therefore, to the divine Spouse of our souls, that He may accept it as helping Him to save immortal souls—our own included.

How merciful the good God is, always "fitting the back to the burden"—if not vice-versa, as is often the case.

The world is full of misunderstanding, but God often uses its mistakes to correct us and to give us the right outlook on life and its eternal destiny.

The Christian virtue of holy resignation [to the will of God] brings astonishing results in this life and an ineffable crown in eternity.

How merciful the good God is in letting us now and then run up against a snag of some kind, that halts us for at least a moment of reflection on the real purpose of our existence as rational creatures: eternity in God.

In the crosses of life that come to us, Jesus offers us opportunities to help Him redeem the world. Let us profit by His generosity.

My pain was excruciating, and though I tried to thank God for it, my principal prayer was: "God help me!"

We should make a virtue of earthly deprivations, by offering them all to our heavenly Father in union with Jesus, who said: "The Son of Man has nowhere to lay His head."

MARY AND THE SAINTS

Perhaps there is no more beautiful example of confidence in God than that of Mary—God's living tabernacle—and St. Joseph seeking an abode wherein to give us salvation.

How little we realize what a benefit it is that we taste sorrow now and then. Get acquainted with the Queen of Martyrs—God's Mother suffering—and you will learn something of how we ought to love sorrow and pains in this life.

Learn to know Mary that you may love heaven and heavenly things.

Studying Mary's life is learning to love God in His works and in His masterpiece.

The Blessed Virgin Mary! Next to Jesus Himself, and always with Him, may she ever be our refuge and our stay during this pilgrimage on earth.

Mary is the Mother of God, and by His divine wisdom, power, and merciful condescension, the Blessed Mother of redeemed humanity, therefore our Blessed Mother also.

How pleasant the glorified memory of the saints in heaven must be, who have finally triumphed over the world, the flesh, and the devil.

DEATH, HEAVEN, AND ETERNITY

Life is the vestibule to eternity.

Death can be very beautiful—like a wedding—if we make it so.

Death is the climax of humiliation, when we must finally give up all and turn all over to God.

Heaven—where love of God and our neighbor is the life and very soul of society and association, where hopeful faith has merged into eternal charity.

Many are the rainbows, the sunbursts, the gentle breezes—and the hail-storms—we are liable to meet before, by the grace of God, we shall be able to tumble into our graves with the confidence of tired children into their places of peaceful slumber.

Let us thank God ahead of time for whatever He foresees is pleasing to Him, leaving everything at His divine disposal, including—with all its circumstances—when, where, and how He may be pleased to dispose the events of our death.

Oh, if we could peek into eternity occasionally during our earthly existence, how different would be our appreciation!

Eternal life: passing from time to eternity, from transitory struggling for existence common to mortals, to the destiny we trust, where anxiety and struggling for existence give place to confidence and union with every ideal ever dreamed of.

Let us prepare for our final moment on earth by patient suffering, prayer, and the sacraments; then we will receive with joyful countenance the final call of the Divine Lover, the Bridegroom of our souls, and gently pass into eternity.

The great lesson God wants us to learn on our pilgrimage here is appreciation for life eternal He has waiting for us.

May God Himself be your reward and final crown, as He is for all who by His holy grace shall persevere.

Like the flowers of autumn, we bloom and shortly fade, but our soul will continue and finally claim our whole risen self.

Only in heaven will humanity's redemption—that great mystery of Love—be understood.

For the Christian to view the passing of a loved one only through the lenses of the worldly wisdom—which so sadly excludes faith in God and, consequently, confidence in a favorable hereafter—would be a sad misfortune.

There is nothing in nature or visible creation, however sublime, but what is simply a shadow, a counterpart, of the supernatural.

Courage, therefore, and with the soul's eye fixed on the goal of eternity, struggle on.

GRATITUDE AND APPRECIATION

Gratitude is the first sign of a thinking, rational creature. Poor humanity's sorrow: ingratitude.

Would that we were appreciative as we ought to be! How happy we would be simply in our creation and the faculties we are endowed with and the divine promises of eternal reward.

To know is to appreciate. God Himself can be appreciated and loved only inasmuch as He is known.

To know and appreciate is to advance in the one science necessary: sanctity.

God Himself is the principal reward even here, for each one of us, inasmuch as we learn to appreciate, inasmuch as we put on Christian gratitude.

Be sure, if the enemy of our soul is pleased at anything in us, it is ingratitude of whatever kind. Why? Ingratitude leads to so many breaks with God and our neighbor.

Humanity's outstanding weakness seems to be a thoughtless want of appreciation for the uncountable blessings by which Almighty God is always surrounding it.

Gratitude is one of the very surest indications of intelligence, and atheism is the blackest ingratitude possible.

There is nothing more rational in reason than to love God. By stifling reason and gratitude, sin begets atheism, which is the unqualified climax of intellectual insanity, of moral degeneracy, of moral blasphemy.

Rightly ordered charity is that I should never forget that the primary purpose of my creation and existence as a rational creature is to recognize and know, to appreciate and love—with an intelligent, personal, and grateful love—my God, my Creator, my Redeemer, my Sanctifier.

Let us thank God for the privilege of being made to resemble His Divine Majesty.

Notes

All notes refer to unpublished sources that are housed at the Capuchin Vice-Postulation Archives, Detroit, Michigan. These sources were used with the permission of the Father Solanus Guild.

Abbreviations
CW: Collected Writings of Fr. Solanus Casey SC: Solanus Casey
Test.: Testimony
VPA: Vice-Postulation Archives
WR: Written Reports

One: Family Roots and Formative Years
1. SC to Fr. Maurice Casey, 2 April 1946, CW (I), 158.
2. SC to Margaret T. LeDoux, 1 April 1930, CW (I), 142.

Three: The Capuchins Welcome a New Man
1. Notebook 9, CW (I), 5.
2. Documents File, VPA.
3. Interview with Fr. Boniface Goldhausen, OFM Cap, in 1970, VPA.
4. Documents File, VPA.

Four: The Simplex Priest
1. CW (II), 135.
2. Notebook 12, CW, Appendix III, 31, 27, 28, 23.
3. Notebook 12, CW, Appendix III, 47.

Five: The Seraphic Mass Association
1. Notebook 1, CW (III), 1, 3, 4, 5, 7.
2. Notebook 1, CW (III), 21.
3. Notebook 9, CW (I), 5.
4. Documents File, VPA.

SIX: MINISTRY IN DETROIT

1. SC to Sr. Mary Joseph, 21 May 1945, CW, Appendix I, 9.

2. SC to Mrs. Helena Wilhite, 28 February 1946, CW (I), 132.

SEVEN: "*DEO GRATIAS*"

1. Radio speech, 11 June 1937, CW (I), 94-95.

2. CW (II), 354.

3. CW (I), 286.

EIGHT: WITNESSES TO HOLINESS

1. Test. Fr. Marion Roessler, OFM Cap, Positio (II), 692.

2. Test. Fr. Marion Roessler, OFM Cap, Positio (II), 691-92.

3. SC to Br. Leo Wollenweber, OFM Cap, 28 February 1943, CW (II), 119.

4. Test. Br. Ignatius Milne, OFM Cap, Positio (II), 15.

TEN: SECRETARIES AND OTHER COLLEAGUES

1. Interview with Br. Booker Ashe, OFM Cap, 21 March 1980, WR, VPA.

2. Test. Br. Gabriel Badalamenti, TOSF, Positio (II), 192.

3. Test. Mr. James Maher, Positio (II), 255.

4. SC to Sr. Mary Bernice, 30 January 1955, CW (II), 351.

5. SC, "Essay on Atheism," CW (II), 165.

6. SC to Mr. Philip R. O'Brien, 20 August 1952, CW (II), 326.

7. SC, "Essay Proposition," CW (II), 267-68.

ELEVEN: THE SACRIFICE OF SELF

1. SC to Rt. Rev. Edward Casey, 14 March 1957, CW (I), 195.

2. Report of Rev. Michael Dalton, 20 November 1977, WR, VPA.

EPILOGUE: THE CAUSE FOR CANONIZATION

1. Document I, Testimonial, 3 August 1957, Positio (I), 290.

2. Document II, newspaper clipping, 1 August 1957, Positio (I), 291.

3. The Messenger 21:2 (February 1958): 40, VPA.

4. Document III, Fr. Benignus of Sant' Ilario, 12 February 1958, Positio (I), 292.

5. Rev. Peter Gumpel, SJ, Relator, Positio (I), 3.

6. Test. Fr. Blase Gitzen, OFM Cap., Positio (II), 322.

A Chronology of the Life of
Fr. Solanus Casey, OFM Cap

1870

November 25—Born Bernard Francis Casey near Prescott, Wisconsin.

December 18—Baptized at St. Joseph Mission Church in Prescott, Wisconsin.

1883

Received First Holy Communion at St Patrick's Church in Hudson, Wisconsin.

Confirmed by Archbishop Thomas L. Grace of St. Paul-Minneapolis at St. Michael's Church in Stillwater, Minnesota.

1887

Completed District School at Burkhardt, Wisconsin. 1887–89 Lived and worked in Stillwater, Minnesota.

1890

Worked in Superior, Wisconsin, on the new electric streetcars.

1892–96

Studied at St. Francis de Sales Seminary of Milwaukee, Wisconsin.

1896

November 19—Received letter of acceptance from the Capuchins at St. Bonaventure Monastery in Detroit, Michigan.

December 8—Heard call to religious life as a Capuchin at close of Novena for the Immaculate Conception in Sacred Heart Church in Superior, Wisconsin.

December 24—Arrived at St. Bonaventure Monastery in Detroit, Michigan.

1897
January 14—Invested as a Capuchin novice and given the name Francis Solanus.

1898
July 21—Made simple profession in Detroit and then began studies at St. Francis Capuchin Monastery in Milwaukee, Wisconsin.

1901
July 21—Made solemn profession of vows at St. Francis Capuchin Monastery in Milwaukee.

1903
December 8—Ordained a subdeacon at St. Francis de Sales Seminary Chapel in Milwaukee.

1904
March 20—Ordained a deacon at St. Francis Capuchin Church in Milwaukee.
July 24—Ordained a priest at St. Francis Capuchin Church by Archbishop Sebastian Messmer of Milwaukee.
July 31—Celebrated his first Holy Mass at St. Joseph Church in Appleton, Wisconsin.
August 4—Arrived at Sacred Heart Friary in Yonkers, New York—his first assignment.

1913
October 6—Attended his parents' golden wedding anniversary celebration in Seattle, Washington.

1915

September 9—Death of his father, Bernard James Casey, in Seattle, Washington, aged 75.

1918

May 2—Death of his mother, Ellen Murphy Casey, in Seattle, Washington, aged 74.

July—Transferred to Our Lady of Sorrows Parish in New York, New York.

1921

October 25—Transferred to Our Lady of Angels Parish in Harlem, New York.

1923

November 8—Began keeping a record of "favors" noted after enrollment in the Seraphic Mass Association as directed by his provincial superior.

1924

August 1—Arrived at St. Bonaventure Monastery in Detroit as the new porter.

1929

July 28—Celebrated his twenty-fifth jubilee of ordination at St. Bonaventure's in Detroit.

1931

December—Appointed delegate for the Seraphic Mass Association. Held this office until 1955.

1937

August 11—Journeyed to Superior, Wisconsin, for the twenty-fifth jubilee of his brother, Msgr. Edward Casey, and then to Prescott, Wisconsin, for the jubilee of their old parish, St. Joseph's.

1945

June—Attended the first Mass celebration of his nephew, Fr. John McCluskey, SJ, in Seattle, Washington.

July 23—Transferred to St. Michael's Parish in Brooklyn, New York.

1946

April 25—Transferred to St. Felix Friary in Huntington, Indiana, for semiretirement.

1947

January 28—Celebrated his golden jubilee as a Capuchin at St. Bonaventure's in Detroit.

1953

January 22—Received letter of commendation from the Capuchin Minister General for his many years of work for the Seraphic Mass Association.

1954

July 28—Celebrated the golden jubilee of his ordination at St. Mary's Church in Huntington, Indiana.

1956

January 12—Was brought back to Detroit for medical treatment and transferred to St. Bonaventure's in May.

1957

January 14—In a private celebration, renewed his vows on the sixtieth anniversary of his profession.

June 28—Offered Mass for the last time, at St. Bonaventure Monastery.

July 2—Returned to St. John Hospital in Detroit.

July 31—Peacefully gave up his soul to God at 11:00 a.m. with the prayer "I give my soul to Jesus Christ."

August 3—Buried from St. Bonaventure's Chapel, after two days' lying in state, and laid to rest in the friary cemetery.

1960

July 31—Organization of the Father Solanus Guild with approval of the Capuchin Provincial Superiors.

1966

October 4—Beginning of cause of canonization for Fr. Solanus with appointment of a Vice-Postulator.

1983

September 23—Opening of diocesan investigation on the life and virtues of the Servant of God Solanus Casey, by the archbishop of Detroit, Edmund C. Szoka.

1987

July 8—Exhumation of the body of Solanus Casey for canonical examination and reinterment in the north transept of St. Bonaventure Church.

1992

October 10—Presentation of the three-volume positio on the life and virtues of Solanus Casey to the Congregation for the Causes of the Saints.

1995

July 11—Declared Venerable Solanus Casey by Pope John Paul II with the promulgation of the Decree of Virtue.

2017

May 4—Pope Francis announces plan for beatification of Fr. Solanus
November 18—Fr. Solanus is beatified and is now known as Blessed Solanus Casey. Memorial feast day set as July 31.

Bibliography

Derum, James Patrick. *The Porter of St. Bonaventure's.* Detroit: Fidelity Press, 1968, 279 pp. The eighth printing was in 1987. This popular biography has been a valuable means of spreading Fr. Solanus's story far and wide. Mr. Derum spent about seven years on his research. He had access to Solanus's letters and notebooks, and he personally interviewed many people who had experienced his help.

One very important source of information was his eight days of conversations with Msgr. Edward Casey, Solanus's last surviving brother. Msgr. Casey even took Mr. Derum over the various farmlands in Wisconsin where the Caseys had lived and related many stories of their home life. This biography is the only source for many of the details of Fr. Solanus's early life before he became a Capuchin.

An Italian translation of Derum's book by P. Roberto Lecchini, *Solano Casey, Il Portinaio Del Convento*, was published at Padua, Italy, 1983, 200 pp.

Other Works on Solanus Casey

Garrity, Leona. *The Man of Faith.* Printed in the Capuchin Annual, Dublin, Ireland, 1971, 20 pp. Mrs. Garrity gathered much of her information from interviews with people who had known and talked with Fr. Solanus during his ministry in Detroit. She also had access to the archives of the Vice-Postulator. Her account includes some reports of favors that Fr. Solanus attributed to enrollment in the Seraphic Mass Association, as recorded in his notebooks.

Crosby, Michael, O.F.M. Cap. *Thank God Ahead of Time*. Cincinnati: Franciscan Media, 2009. This more complete biography is an in-depth study of the spirituality of Fr. Solanus Casey based upon many of his own writings. Fr. Crosby, a Capuchin, writes from the perspective of the Franciscan heritage. He had access to much new material not known to earlier biographers. His work is well documented with many notes and a complete index.

Odell, Catherine M. *Father Solanus*. Huntington, Ind.: Our Sunday Visitor, 1988, 228 pp. When this author lived in Huntington twenty years after the death of Fr. Solanus Casey, people still remembered him and recounted their own stories about him. This inspired Mrs. Odell to tell his story from a fresh viewpoint relevant to the times in which he lived. While many facts are borrowed from the biographies of Derum and Crosby, Mrs. Odell has included more material about the cause of Fr. Solanus. The final section contains some excerpts from Solanus' writings, and the book is fully annotated.

Crosby, Michael, O.F.M. Cap., ed. *Solanus Casey: The Official Account of a Virtuous American Life*. New York: Crossroad, 2000, 275 pp. This book contains in one volume the first and third volumes of the official *positio* on the life and virtues of the Servant of God Solanus Casey.

Casey, St. Bernadine, S.N.J.M., ed. *Letters From Solanus Casey, O.F.M., Cap*. Detroit, Mich.: Father Solanus Guild, 2000, 306 pp. Fr. Solanus's niece compiled this critical selection of letters written by Solanus Casey to some family members and others who asked for his advice and prayers. She includes biographical sketches of his parents, grandparents, and siblings.

Three anthologies, each with a chapter or two devoted to Fr. Solanus, have appeared since 1982:

Tylenda, Joseph N., ed. *Portraits in American Sanctity*. Quincy, Ill.: Franciscan Press, 1982.

Baldwin, Robert. *The Healers*. Huntington, Ind.: Our Sunday Visitor, 1986.

Treece, Patricia. *Nothing Short of a Miracle*. Huntington, Ind.: Our Sunday Visitor, 1988.

Many other short sketches of Fr. Solanus's life have been printed and distributed since 1976. Short pamphlets such as *Fr. Capuchin*, 1976; *The Message of Father Solanus Casey, Capuchin*, 1977; *Thanks Be to God*, 1978; and *The Doorkeeper*, 1987, have been printed—more than twenty thousand copies of each. *Fr. Capuchin* was translated into Spanish in 1982 and printed in Managua, Nicaragua.

Besides the many tributes to Fr. Solanus in the daily newspapers at the time of his death in 1957, many other articles have since then reported the significant steps in the movement for his beatification. Throughout the United States and in some foreign countries, many newspapers and magazines have printed his story—especially in the states of Michigan, Wisconsin, Minnesota, New York, and Indiana, where about fifty articles have appeared since 1969. Interest in the life of Fr. Solanus and his good work continues to spread far and wide.

About the Author

Brother Leo Wollenweber, OFM Cap, was a vice-postulator for the cause of Solanus Casey. A native of Detroit, Michigan, he was a Capuchin Brother for seventy-two years. He died on October 5, 2012 at the age of ninety-five and is buried at St. Bonaventure's Monastery in Detroit.